OLSAT™
GRADE 4 & GRADE 5
TEST PREP

OLSAT®
GRADE 4 & GRADE 5
TEST PREP
Level E

Gateway Gifted Resources™
www.GatewayGifted.com

PLEASE LEAVE US A REVIEW!

Thank you for selecting this book. We are a family-owned publishing company - a consortium of educators, book designers, illustrators, parents, and kid-testers.

We would be thrilled if you left us a quick review on the website where you purchased this book!

The Gateway Gifted Resources™ Team
www.GatewayGifted.com

TABLE OF CONTENTS

INTRODUCTION

ABOUT THIS BOOK: This book helps prepare kids for the OLSAT® Level E, a test given to fourth and fifth graders. Not only will this publication help prepare kids for the OLSAT®, these logic-based exercises may also be used for other gifted test preparation and as critical thinking exercises. This book has four parts.

1. Introduction: About this book & the OLSAT®, Test-Taking Tips, Points Tracking, and Question Examples

2. Practice Test 1 (Workbook Format): These pages are designed similarly to content tested in the OLSAT®'s 15 test question types. Questions are grouped by question type, so that your student can more easily comprehend question material.

Unless your student already has experience with OLSAT® prep materials, you should complete Practice Test 1 (Workbook Format) together with no time limit. **Before doing this section with your student, read the Question Examples & Explanations.**

3. Practice Test 2 & Practice Test 3: These help kids develop critical thinking and test-taking skills. It provides an introduction to standardized testing in a relaxed manner (parents provide guidance if needed) and an opportunity for kids to focus on a group of questions for a longer time period. This part is also a way for parents to identify points of strength/ challenges.

Questions in Practice Test 2 & 3 are not grouped by question type. When your student takes the test, questions will most likely not be grouped by question type.

4. Answer Keys: This has the answers to Practice Test 1, 2, and 3 as well as brief answer explanations.

ABOUT THE OLSAT® LEVEL E

- The OLSAT® Level E is given to kids in fourth and fifth grade.
- It has 72 questions in multiple choice format.
- The test lasts approximately one hour.
- Schools use the test for admittance to gifted/advanced programs.
- Questions are different than those found on typical grade level quizzes, tests, and standardized testing.
- Here are the three OLSAT® Level E question types and corresponding question sections:

   -Verbal: Antonyms, Sentence Completion, Sentence Arrangement, Arithmetic Reasoning, Verbal Analogies, Verbal Classification, Logical Selection, Word/Letter Matrix, and Inference

   -Non Verbal: Figure Analogies, Figure Series, Pattern Matrix

   -Quantitative: Numeric Inferences, Numeric Matrix, Numeric Series

ABOUT OLSAT® TESTING PROCEDURES: These vary by school. Tests may be given individually or in a group. These tests may be used as the single factor for admission to gifted programs, or they may be used in combination with IQ tests or as part of a student "portfolio." They are used by some schools together with tests like Iowa Assessments™. Check with your testing site to determine its specific testing procedures.

QUESTION NOTE: Because each student has different cognitive abilities, the questions in this book are at varied skill levels. The exercises may or may not require a great deal of parental guidance to complete, depending on your student's abilities, prior test prep experience, or prior testing experience. Most sections of Practice Test 1 begin with a relatively easy question. We suggest always completing at least the first question together, ensuring your student is not confused about what the question asks or with the directions.

SCORING NOTE: Check with your school for its scoring procedure and admissions requirements. Here is a general summary of the OLSAT® scoring process. First, your child's raw score is established. This is the number of questions correctly answered. Points are not deducted for questions answered incorrectly. Next, this score is compared to other test-takers of his/her same age group to then calculate your student's percentile rank. If your student achieved the percentile rank of 98%, then (s)he scored as well as or better than 98% of test-takers. Note that a percentile rank "score" cannot be obtained from our practice material. This material has not been given to a large enough sample of test-takers to develop any kind of base score necessary for percentile rank calculations.

TEST-TAKING TIPS
• **Be sure your student looks carefully at each answer choice.** OLSAT® questions can be quite challenging. Even if your student thinks (s)he knows the answer - (s)he should look at each choice.
•**Test-takers receive points for the number of correct answers.** If your student says that (s)he does not know the answer, (s)he should first eliminate answers that are clearly incorrect. Guess instead of leaving a question blank.
• **In Practice Test 1, go through the exercises together by talking about them:** what the exercise is asking the student to do and what makes the answer choices correct/incorrect. This will familiarize them with working through exercises and will help to develop a process of elimination (getting rid of incorrect answer choices).
• **Remember common sense tips like getting enough sleep.** It has been scientifically proven that kids perform below their grade level when tired. **Provide a breakfast for sustained energy and concentration** (complex carbohydrates and protein; avoid foods/drinks high in sugar). Have them use the restroom prior to the test.

POINTS TRACKING
To increase student engagement and to add an incentive to complete book exercises, a game theme accompanies this book. As your student completes the three Practice Tests, (s)he earns 1 point per page. After completing all pages, they will have earned 68 points. Some parents may want to offer a special treat as well for completion, although this is at the parent's discretion.

WE NEED YOUR HELP!

We've got a challenge for you! Are you up for it?

This book is filled with mind-bending, challenging questions, and we need your help to answer them.

For every page you do, you earn 1 point.

So far, the highest score anyone has ever earned is 68 points. Do you have what it takes to earn 68? Use the space below to track your points.

The questions start on page 6. Your parent (or other adult) will let you know what you need to do. Remember to:

*   pay close attention to each word (or number) in the question
*   look carefully at all choices before choosing an answer
*   keep trying even if some questions are hard

CAN
YOU
EARN
68
POINTS?

POINTS TRACKING

Date	Points	Date	Points	Date	Points
_____	_____	_____	_____	_____	_____
_____	_____	_____	_____	_____	_____

QUESTION EXAMPLES & EXPLANATIONS

This section introduces the 15 question types on the OLSAT® Level E using basic examples and explanations.

VERBAL SECTION

1. Antonyms
Directions: Read the sentence and choose which word is the opposite of the word in quotation marks.

The opposite of "best" is _____.

A. slow   B. bad   C. worst   D. great

The opposite of "best" is "worst." This section tests a student's vocabulary and their ability to reason and recognize a word's true opposite. In the example above, some students may choose "bad," when "worst" is actually the true opposite. Be sure to carefully go through the choices to pick the true opposite.

2. Sentence Completion
Directions: Read the sentence. There is a missing word. Which answer choice goes best in the sentence?

If you are not _____ with the vase, it will break.

A. careless   B. careful   C. clear   D. risky

The answer is B. Here, be sure to pay attention to each word in the sentence. After choosing your answer, reread the sentence together with your answer choice. Pay attention for "negative" words like "not." Also pay attention for "contrasting" words like "however," "but," "despite," that can be used to show contrasting ideas in sentences.

3. Sentence Arrangement
Directions: The words below need to be arranged to make the best sentence. Which letter would the first word of the sentence begin with? Here are the words:

yummy   for   waited   puppies   a   treat   the   two

A. P   B. T   C. W   D. Y

The correct sentence is: The two puppies waited for a yummy treat. The answer is B. Here are some tips.

1- Finding the main subject and verb will help you establish the basic structure. First, identify the verb(s). This will give you a clue to the subject. Then, try to identify the subject. Some sentences will have more than one noun that could be the subject. If there is more than one noun, test each one.
2- Group related words: Identify phrases or groups of words that belong together (e.g., adjectives with nouns, adverbs with verbs). This can help you see how parts of the sentence connect.
3- Look for clues: Some sentences may have words that indicate time (e.g., "yesterday," "now"), conjunctions (e.g., "and," "but"), or prepositions (e.g., "in," "on") that provide context and help you organize the sentence.

4. Arithmetic Reasoning   Directions: Read the question then choose your answer.

Julia and Mike had pizza for lunch. Julia ate 7 slices. Mark ate 2 more slices than Julia. How many slices did they eat all together?

A. 9   B. 7   C. 16   D. 12

First, find the number Mark ate. He ate 2 more than Julia, so 2 + 7 = 9. Mark at 9 slices. Julia ate 7 slices. So, 9+7 = 16. These questions are not a test solely of math abilities. They are an assessment of your student's ability to read word problems, turn the words into equations, and solve the equations.

5. Logical Selection   Directions: Read the sentence and choose which word best completes the sentence.

A lake must have _____.

A. boats   B. fish   C. swimmers   D. water

The answer is water. Here, you need to use logic and reasoning to figure out which choice is the only one that is truly needed.

6. Verbal Analogies
Directions: Look at the first set of words. Try to figure out how they belong together. Next, look at the second set of words. The answer is missing. Figure out which answer choice would make the second set go together in the same way that the first set goes together.

toe > foot : petal > ?   A. stem   B. bee   C. leg   D. flower

The answer is D. Here are some strategies to help arrive at the correct answer:
• Try to come up with a "rule" describing how the first set goes together. Take this rule, apply it to the first word in the second set. Which answer choice makes the second set follow the same "rule?" If more than one choice works, you need a more specific rule. Here, a "rule" for the first set is that "the first word (toe) is part of the second word (foot)." In the next set, using this rule, "flower" is the answer. A petal is part of a flower.
• Another strategy is to come up with a sentence describing how the first set of words go together. A sentence would be: A toe is part of a foot. Then, take this sentence and apply it to the word in the second set: A petal is part of a ?. Figure out which answer choice would best complete the sentence. (It would be "flower.")
• Do not choose a word simply because it has to do with the first set. For example, choice A ("stem") has to do with a petal, but does not follow the rule.

Here are more simple examples. Read the "Question" then "Answer Choices" to your student. Which choice goes best? (The answer is underlined.)

Analogy Logic	Question	Answer Choices (Answer is Underlined)			
• Antonyms	On is to Off -as- Hot is to ?	Warm	Sun	Cold	Oven
• Synonyms	Big is to Large -as- Horrible is to ?	Tired	Stale	Sour	Awful
• Whole: Part	Tree is to Branch -as- House is to ?	Street	Apartment	Room	Home
• Degree	Good is to Excellent -as- Tired is to ?	Boring	Exhausted	Drowsy	Slow
• Object: Location	Sun is to Sky -as- Swing is to ?	Playground	Monkey Bars	Sidewalk	Grass
• Object: Creator	Painting is to Artist -as- Furniture is to ?	Carpenter	Tool	Chair	Potter
• Object: Container	Ice Cube is to Ice Tray -as- Flower is to ?	Petal	Vase	Smell	Florist
• Object: 3D Shape	Ball is to Sphere -as- Dice is to ?	Line	Square	Cone	Cube
• Object: Location Used	Jet is to Sky -as- Canoe is to ?	Boat	Paddle	Water	Sail

7. Verbal Classification
Directions: These words all go together in a certain way except for one. Which word does not go with the others?

A. fork   B. chopsticks   C. knife   D. meat   E. spoon

Here, D is the answer. All the others are utensils used for eating. However, meat is a kind of food. Even though meat has to do with food, it is not like the others.

Try to come up with a "rule" describing how the words are alike, except for one. If more than one choice does not follow the rule, then try a more specific rule. More examples are on the next page.

Read the list of 5 words to your student, then ask which does not belong.
The gray text lists the question's logic. The underlined text is the word that does not belong.

• functions and uses of common objects (i.e., writing and drawing / measuring / cutting / drinking / eating)
Fork / Chopsticks / Knife / Meat / Spoon   (Utensils Used For Eating)

• location of common objects
Refrigerator / Shower / Cabinet / Table / Oven   (Found In Kitchens)

• appearance of common objects (i.e., color; objects in pairs; objects with stripes vs. spots; object's shape)
Box / Baseball / Sphere / Basketball / Globe   (Round)

• characteristics of common objects (i.e., hot, cold)
Ice / Igloo / Popsicle / Coffee / Snowman   (Cold Things)

• animal/human homes
Aquarium / Fish / Barn / Nest / Beehive   (Animal Homes)

• animal types
Leopard / Cheetah / Lion / Tiger / Monkey   (Cats)

• natural habitats
Swamp / River / Mountain / Ocean / Pond   (Water)

• food types
Cake / Bread / Donut / Syrup / Cookie   (Baked Foods)

• food growing location (i.e., on a tree, under the ground as a root, or on a vine)
Melon / Potato / Carrot / Onion / Radish   (Root Vegetables)

• professions, community helpers
Doctor / Teacher / Wizard / Fireman / Vet   (Community Helpers)

• clothing (i.e., in what weather it's worn; on what body part it's worn)
Crown / Cowboy Hat / Cap / Gloves / Helmet   (Worn On Head)

• transportation (i.e., where things travel, land/water/air; do they have wheels?)
Cruise Ship / Canoe / Car / Yacht / Kayak   (Travel On Water)

8. Letter Matrix / Word Matrix

Directions: Look at what is in the box. You will see either words or simply letters. They go together in a certain way. Then, look at the answer choices. What answer choice would go where the question mark is?

e e	t r	t r e e
l l	c a	?

A. call   B. cart   C. trace   D. eel

Here, take the 2 letters in the second set of letters "tr" and put them in front of the 2 letters in the first set "ee": tr + ee = tree. With the bottom row, do the same: ca + ll = call. Therefore, choice A is the answer.

Note that some questions will have words (not letters). An example in Practice Test 1 includes words, for your reference. With these types of questions (questions that include words), the pattern involves words that are in alphabetical order or words that are opposites.

9. Inferences

Directions: Read the sentences. Based on the information given in the sentences, choose the correct answer choice.

Ana runs faster than Mia. Mia runs faster than Lily. Which one is true?

Ⓐ Ana runs slower than Lily.

Ⓑ Mia runs faster than Ana.

Ⓒ Lily runs faster than Ana.

Ⓓ Ana runs faster than Lily.

Ⓔ Lily and Mia run at the same speed.

In this simple example, carefully follow the logic given in the statements. First statement: "Ana runs faster than Mia." This means Ana is faster than Mia (A > M). Second statement: "Mia runs faster than Lily." This means Mia is faster than Lily (M > L). Combine the two pieces of information. Ana is faster than Mia, and Mia is faster than Lily (A > M > L). Therefore, Ana must also be faster than Lily, because Ana is the fastest of all three. Next, carefully read each answer choice to find which one matches the information you just evaluated. The only answer choice that is true is choice D, "Ana runs faster than Lily."

NON-VERBAL SECTION

10. Figure Analogies

Directions: The pictures inside the top boxes go together in a certain way. Which answer choice goes with the picture in the bottom box like the pictures in the top boxes do? (The word "picture" here refers to a "figure" that can consist of shapes, lines, etc.)

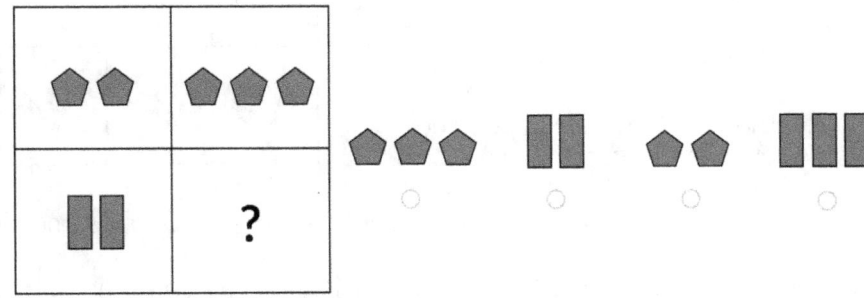

Explanation Come up with a "rule" describing how the top set is related. This shows how the left box "changes" into the right box. On the left are 2 pentagons. On the right are 3 pentagons. The rule/change is that one more of the same kind of shape was added. On the bottom are 2 rectangles. The first choice is incorrect because it shows 3 pentagons - not the same shapes as the bottom box. The second choice is incorrect - it only shows 2 rectangles. The third choice is incorrect - it has 2 pentagons. The last choice is correct - there are 3 rectangles (1 more of the same shapes that were in the left box).

Here are 12 <u>basic</u> Figure Analogy "changes."

1. Color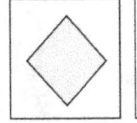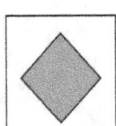

2. Size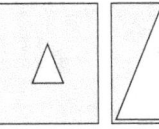

3. Amount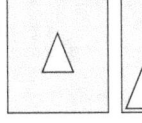

4. Color Reversal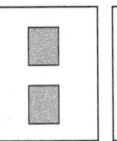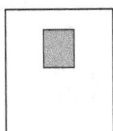

5. Whole to Part

6. Shape Sides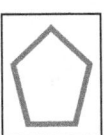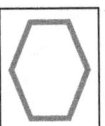

The list continues on the next page.

Basic Figure Analogy "changes," continued

7. Rotation: 90° clockwise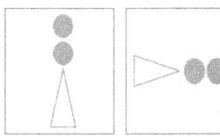

8. Rotation: 90° counter-clockwise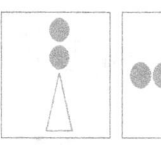

9. Line Direction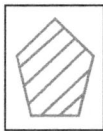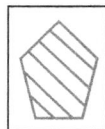

10. Flip/ Mirror Image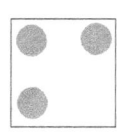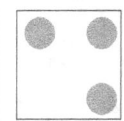

11. Two Changes: Rotation & Quantity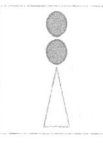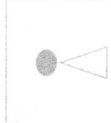

12. Two Changes: Rotation & Color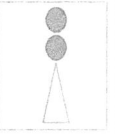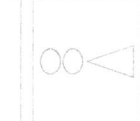

11. Pattern Matrices

Directions: Look at the pictures inside the boxes. They make a pattern. Look at the last box. It is empty. Look next to the boxes at the row of pictures. Which one should go inside the empty box in the bottom row?

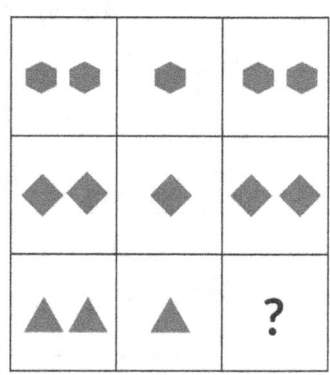  

Explanation Across the top row, here is the pattern: 2 shapes - 1 shape - 2 shapes (the same kind of shape). The middle row has this pattern also. In the bottom row, we see 2 shapes - 1 shape - and... what would be the answer? It would be 2 shapes of the same kind of shape (triangles). The answer is D.

Common logic themes found in Figure Analogies are also found in Pattern Matrices.

12. Figure Series

Directions: In this row of boxes, the pictures belong together in some way. Another picture should go inside the empty box. Which picture in the row of answer choices should go in this empty box?

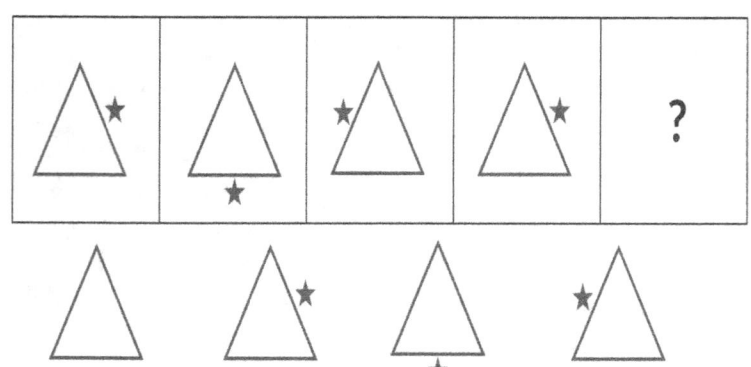

Explanation Here, figure out the pattern inside the boxes. First, the star is on the right side of the triangle, then it moves to the bottom of the triangle, then to the left side, and then to the right side. Where would the star move next? It would move to the bottom, Choice C. (The star moves clockwise around the triangle's sides.)

Common logic found in Figure Analogies is also found in Figure Series questions.

QUANTITATIVE SECTION

13. Numeric Matrix

Directions: Look at the numbers inside the boxes. They go together in a certain way. Which answer choice would go inside the empty box in the bottom row?

2	3	4
7	8	9
12	13	?

Ⓐ 14   Ⓑ 15   Ⓒ 18   Ⓓ 11

Here, try to come up with a "rule" that applies to the numbers going across the rows. There is also a "rule" that applies going down the columns.

Going across the rows, you see that the "rule" is "add 1."
Going down the columns, you see that the "rule" is "add 5."

Given this, the answer is A.

14. Numeric Inferences

Directions: Look at the first two sets of numbers. Come up with a rule that both of these sets follow. Take this rule to figure out which answer choice goes in the place of the question mark.

[10 →5]   [8 →4]   [14 →?]   A.2   B.7   C.28   D.16   E.1

Come up with a rule to explain how the first number "changes" into the second. It could use addition, subtraction, multiplication, or division. Write the rule by each pair. Make sure it works with both pairs. The rule is "÷ by 2", so 7 is the answer.

15. Numeric Series

Directions: Which answer choice would continue the pattern?

15   13   11   9   7   ?   A.1   B.3   C.5   D.6   E.4

The numbers make a pattern. To help figure out the pattern, notice the difference between each number and the next. In this basic example, the pattern is: -2.

In easier questions, the difference between all consecutive numbers is the same (i.e., the difference between 15 & 13 = 2 and between 13 & 11 = 2). However, sometimes the difference will not continuously repeat itself, as in these examples:

9	8	6	5	3	2	?	The pattern is: -1, -2, -1, -2, etc. & the answer is 0.
1	2	4	7	11	16	?	The pattern is: +1, +2, +3, +4, etc. & the answer is 22.
4	5	9	4	5	9	?	The pattern is: 4-5-9 & the answer is 4.
0	10	0	20	0	30	?	Note: this pattern "skips." Every other number is 0. Also, every other number between a "0" has a pattern of +10 The answer is 0.

-Practice Test 1 (Workbook Format) Begins On The Next Page.-

ANTONYMS

Directions: Read the sentence and choose which answer is the opposite of the word given.

Example

The opposite of entrance is _____.

Ⓐ door   Ⓑ path   Ⓒ exit   Ⓓ gateway   Ⓔ hall

1 **The opposite of blend is _____.**

Ⓐ mix   Ⓑ separate   Ⓒ add   Ⓓ create   Ⓔ improve

2 **The opposite of create is _____.**

Ⓐ rebuild   Ⓑ improve   Ⓒ pause   Ⓓ think   Ⓔ destroy

3 **The opposite of ease is _____.**

Ⓐ difficulty   Ⓑ comfort   Ⓒ joy   Ⓓ lengthy   Ⓔ boring

4 **The opposite of distract is _____.**

Ⓐ disturb   Ⓑ confuse   Ⓒ disrupt   Ⓓ focus   Ⓔ ignore

Example Answer: C (The answers for the rest are in the Answer Key.)

SENTENCE COMPLETION

Directions: Read the sentence. There is a missing word. Look at the row of answer choices below the sentence. Which word would go best in the sentence?

Example

Three examples of _____ include forests, deserts, and savannas.

Ⓐ borders   Ⓑ climates   Ⓒ habitats   Ⓓ maps   Ⓔ plants

5   **If you want to prevent a stomachache, then you should _____ eating too many sweets.**

      Ⓐ keep   Ⓑ appreciate   Ⓒ enjoy   Ⓓ avoid   Ⓔ continue

6   **There was a(n) _____ change in temperature this week that caused all the snow to melt extremely fast.**

      Ⓐ slow   Ⓑ mild   Ⓒ gradual   Ⓓ frigid   Ⓔ abrupt

7   **Despite _____ having enough time to take long vacations, he does go on brief weekend trips.**

      Ⓐ seldom   Ⓑ frequently   Ⓒ always   Ⓓ surely   Ⓔ regularly

8   **The police finally located and _____ the thief resting under a bridge that was _____ as a spot where criminals hide.**

      Ⓐ released, known   Ⓑ secured, crafted   Ⓒ carried, built   Ⓓ congratulated, famed   Ⓔ captured, notorious

Example Answer: C. habitat: an animal or plant's natural home (The answers for the rest are in the Answer Key.)

SENTENCE ARRANGEMENT

Note: Be sure to pay attention to whether you are asked to find the <u>first</u> word of the sentence or the <u>last</u> word of the sentence.

Example

Directions: The words below need to be arranged to make the best sentence. Which letter would the <u>last</u> word of the sentence begin with? Here are the words:

laughed	joke	the	funny	at	a	kids

Ⓐ K   Ⓑ L   Ⓒ F   Ⓓ J   Ⓔ A

9   The words below need to be arranged to make the best sentence. Which letter would the <u>first</u> word of the sentence begin with? Here are the words:

air	the	feathers	have	birds	help	that	in	them	fly

Ⓐ A   Ⓑ F   Ⓒ H   Ⓓ B   Ⓔ I

Example Answer: D: Correct sentence: The kids laughed at a funny joke.
(The answers for the rest are in the Answer Key.)

10   The words below need to be arranged to make the best sentence.
Which letter would the <u>first</u> word of the sentence begin with?
Here are the words:

heat   light   Earth   the   and   provides   sun   to

Ⓐ H   Ⓑ L   Ⓒ E   Ⓓ T   Ⓔ A

11   The words below need to be arranged to make the best sentence.
Which letter would the <u>first</u> word of the sentence begin with?
Here are the words:

attract   magnets   can   iron   metals   like

Ⓐ A   Ⓑ M   Ⓒ C   Ⓓ I   Ⓔ L

12   The words below need to be arranged to make the best sentence.
Which letter would the <u>first</u> word of the sentence begin with?
Here are the words:

toys   everyone   sharing   happy   makes   friends   with

Ⓐ T   Ⓑ S   Ⓒ U   Ⓓ T   Ⓔ H

ARITHMETIC REASONING

Note: The primary skill tested here is <u>not</u> your student's math level. You'll find some questions use quite basic math operations. The primary skill tested here involves taking the words in the math problem, turning the words into the correct math equations, and solving the equations.

Directions: Read the question then choose your answer.

Example 1

Mark had 20 pencils in his backpack. He gave 8 pencils to a friend and lost 4 pencils. How many pencils does Mark have left?

Ⓐ 6   Ⓑ 8   Ⓒ 12   Ⓓ 14   Ⓔ 16

Example 2

Sarah goes for a walk in her neighborhood. She walks 4 miles to the park, then walks 2 miles further to the lake. After spending some time at the lake, she walks 3 miles to the cafe and then another 5 miles home. How many miles did Sarah walk in total?

Ⓐ 10   Ⓑ 12   Ⓒ 14   Ⓓ 16   Ⓔ 18

Example Answers: B. (20 - 8 = 12 pencils left. Then, Mark lost 4 pencils, so: 12 - 4 = 8 pencils left.); C. (To solve this, we need to add up all the distances Sarah walked: 4 + 2 + 3 + 5 = 14 miles.)

13   Jason starts with 100 items. On Monday, he buys 30 items. On Tuesday, he sells 25 items. On Wednesday, he buys 15 more items. On Thursday, he sells 40 items. How many items does Jason have left now?

Ⓐ 70   Ⓑ 80   Ⓒ 90   Ⓓ 100   Ⓔ 110

14   What is eight more than ten times five?

Ⓐ 40   Ⓑ 50   Ⓒ 58   Ⓓ 60   Ⓔ 70

15   In a classroom, there are 8 desks. The teacher places 3 books on each of the first 4 desks and 5 books on each of the remaining 4 desks. How many books did the teacher place in total?

Ⓐ 32   Ⓑ 40   Ⓒ 44   Ⓓ 50   Ⓔ 60

16   What is five more than three times six, minus four?

Ⓐ 9   Ⓑ 14   Ⓒ 17   Ⓓ 19   Ⓔ 22

LOGICAL SELECTION

Directions: Read the sentence and choose which word best completes the sentence.

Tip: Be sure to think carefully about whether or not each answer choice is truly needed.

Example

A car must always have _____.

   Ⓐ a radio   Ⓑ wheels   Ⓒ a trunk   Ⓓ air conditioning   Ⓔ a back seat

17   **A school must always have _____.**

   Ⓐ a cafeteria   Ⓑ students   Ⓒ a library   Ⓓ a playground   Ⓔ computers

18   **A newspaper must always have _____.**

   Ⓐ subscribers   Ⓑ photos   Ⓒ pages   Ⓓ ads   Ⓔ cartoons

19   **A bicycle must always have _____.**

   Ⓐ paint   Ⓑ a bell   Ⓒ a basket   Ⓓ two wheels   Ⓔ a light

20   **A chair must always have _____.**

   Ⓐ a cushion   Ⓑ arms   Ⓒ legs   Ⓓ a back   Ⓔ fabric

Example Answer: B (Every car must have wheels to move. Not all cars have a radio, trunk, air conditioning, or a back seat.)

VERBAL ANALOGIES

Directions: The first set of words goes together in a certain way. Look at the second set of words. The answer is missing. Which answer choice would make the second set go together in the same way that the first set goes together?

Tip: Think of a "rule" or a sentence describing how each pair goes together.

Example

drum → instrument : horse → ?

Ⓐ stable   Ⓑ breed   Ⓒ mammal   Ⓓ pony   Ⓔ cow

21   **letter → word : sentence → ?**

Ⓐ atlas   Ⓑ letters   Ⓒ predicate   Ⓓ subject   Ⓔ paragraph

22   **foot → mile : day → ?**

Ⓐ Monday   Ⓑ year   Ⓒ noon   Ⓓ hour   Ⓔ minute

23   **dishes → cabinet : hay → ?**

Ⓐ barn   Ⓑ harvest   Ⓒ wheat   Ⓓ tractor   Ⓔ field

24   **ceiling → sealing : Greece → ?**

Ⓐ niece   Ⓑ piece   Ⓒ green   Ⓓ grease   Ⓔ greed

Example Answer: C. A drum is a type of instrument. A horse is a type of mammal.

VERBAL CLASSIFICATION

Directions: Which word does not go with the others?

Tips: Figure out how all of the words, except for one, are alike.

Try to come up with a "rule" describing this. Then, take this "rule," and figure out which of the answer choices does not follow it.

If you find that more than one choice does not follow the rule, then try to come up with a rule that is more specific.

The "rule" in the example is: types of large cats.

In the example, a giraffe is not a type of large cat, so choice E (giraffe) is the answer.

Example

Which word does not go with the others?

Ⓐ cougar　　　Ⓑ leopard　　　Ⓒ panther　　　Ⓓ jaguar　　　Ⓔ giraffe

Example Answer: E. cats (The answers for the rest are in the Answer Key.)

25   **Which word does not go with the others?**

Ⓐ heart   Ⓑ organ   Ⓒ stomach   Ⓓ brain   Ⓔ lungs

26   **Which word does not go with the others?**

Ⓐ atlas   Ⓑ dictionary   Ⓒ autobiography   Ⓓ newspaper   Ⓔ legend

27   **Which word does not go with the others?**

Ⓐ base   Ⓑ complete   Ⓒ conclude   Ⓓ end   Ⓔ finish

28   **Which word does not go with the others?**

Ⓐ contrasting   Ⓑ different   Ⓒ prior   Ⓓ unlike   Ⓔ dissimilar

LETTER MATRIX / WORD MATRIX

Directions: Look at what is in the box. You will see either words or simply letters. They go together in a certain way. Then, look at the answer choices. What answer choice would go where the question mark is?

Tips: First, figure out if the things in the boxes are words or simply letters.

Then, see if you can figure out how they go together. First, look across. Across the rows, you see two sets of two letters followed by a word. Look at the top row. In the second set of two letters, you replace the first letter of the second set with the letter "a." Then, you put the letters together. This also works with the bottom row.

If you cannot see how they go together by going across from left to right, then, starting from the first column, look up and down. Example 2 is like this. Going from the top word to the bottom word, you see that the words are in alphabetical order. This "rule" applies for all the words: allow > below > crow > disavow > elbow.

EXAMPLE 1

lo	lf	loaf
to	td	?

Ⓐ tool   Ⓑ tail   Ⓒ toad   Ⓓ toff   Ⓔ tofu

EXAMPLE 2

allow	crow	elbow
below	disavow	?

Ⓐ bow   Ⓑ glow   Ⓒ hollow   Ⓓ follow   Ⓔ narrow

Example Answers: C, D (See explanations above.)

29

pe	ps	pest
mu	ms	?

Ⓐ mist Ⓑ mast Ⓒ mess Ⓓ most Ⓔ must

30

di	dn	dine
hi	hv	?

Ⓐ home Ⓑ hunt Ⓒ hen Ⓓ hive Ⓔ hint

31

so	sm	some
go	gn	?

Ⓐ game Ⓑ gum Ⓒ gone Ⓓ goal Ⓔ give

32

increase	enormous	begin
decrease	minuscule	?

Ⓐ conclude Ⓑ prepare Ⓒ commence Ⓓ announce Ⓔ support

INFERENCES

Directions: Read the sentences. Based on the information given in the sentences, choose the correct answer choice.

Tips:
Be sure to carefully read each sentence.

Pay attention to keywords like these:
- only
- if
- and
- or
- not

Use the given rules to analyze the facts. Then, determine which conditions are true or false based on the sentences in the question. Finally, review the choices and eliminate ones that don't follow the rules described in the sentences in the question.

EXAMPLE

Read the sentences and choose an answer.

Alex will play basketball only if the weather is good. If Alex is tired, he will not go to the gym. Alex is at the gym and is playing basketball. Therefore:

Ⓐ Alex is not tired and the weather is good.

Ⓑ Alex is tired and the weather is good.

Ⓒ Alex is not tired and the weather is bad.

Ⓓ Alex is tired and the weather is bad.

Ⓔ Alex is not tired and the gym is closed.

The sentence states that Alex is playing basketball. If he is playing basketball, that means the weather must be good. The sentence also states that Alex is at the gym. If Alex is at the gym, he must not be tired. We know that he will not go to the gym if he is tired. Therefore, the correct answer is A: "Alex is not tired and the weather is good."

33   **All cats are animals. All tigers are cats. Therefore:**

Ⓐ All animals are tigers.

Ⓑ All animals are cats.

Ⓒ All cats are tigers.

Ⓓ Some cats are not animals.

Ⓔ All tigers are animals and cats.

34   **Liam has fewer books than Oliver. Oliver has more books than Emma. Which of the following is true?**

Ⓐ Emma has the most books.

Ⓑ Emma and Liam have the same number of books.

Ⓒ Oliver has the fewest books.

Ⓓ Oliver has the most books.

Ⓔ Liam has the fewest books.

35   **Mark ran more miles than John. Lisa ran fewer miles than Kevin, but more than Mark. Kevin ran more miles than John. Which of the following is true?**

Ⓐ Kevin ran the second-most miles.

Ⓑ Mark ran the most miles.

Ⓒ John ran the fewest miles.

Ⓓ Lisa ran the fewest miles.

FIGURE ANALOGIES

Directions: Look at the top boxes. The pictures inside belong together in a certain way. Look at the bottom boxes. One is empty. Which answer choice would go with the picture in the bottom box in the same way that the top boxes go together?

Tips: Use the same methodology to complete Figure Analogies as you used for Verbal Analogies.

Work through these together so your student sees how the first set is related.

Together, come up with a "rule" to describe how the first set is related. Then, in the second set, look at the first picture. Take this "rule," use it together with the first picture, and figure out which of the answer choices would follow that same rule.

For answer choices that do not follow this rule, eliminate them. If your student finds that more than one choice follows this rule, then try to come up with a rule that is more specific.

In the example, we see that the outer shape & inner shape switch positions. Also, the inner shape becomes larger and the outer shape becomes smaller.

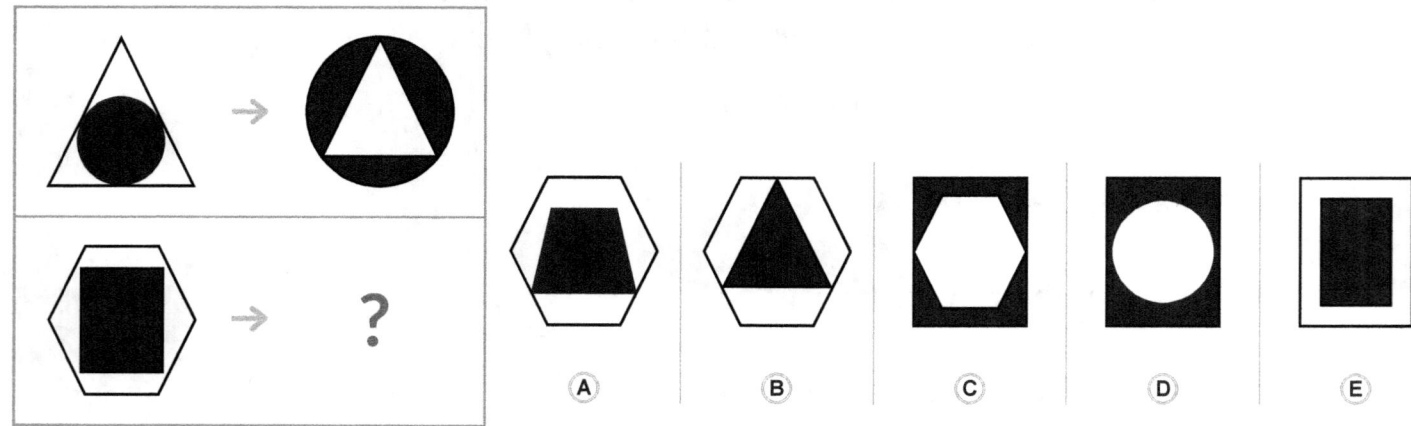

Example Answer: C (See explanation above.)

36

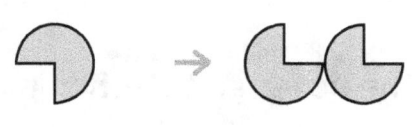

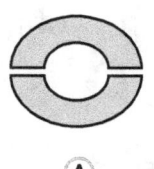    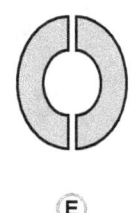

Ⓐ   Ⓑ   Ⓒ   Ⓓ   Ⓔ

37

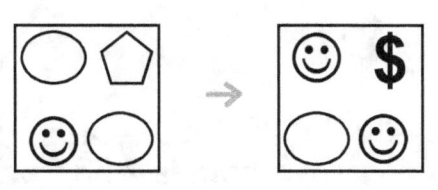

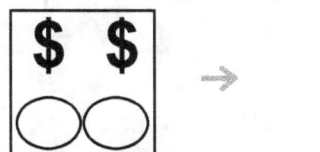

 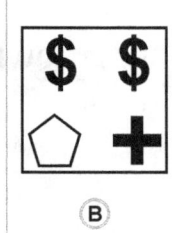 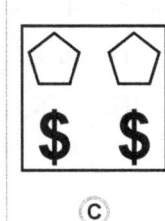 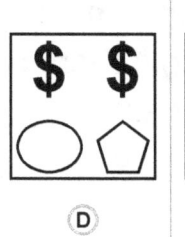 

Ⓐ   Ⓑ   Ⓒ   Ⓓ   Ⓔ

38

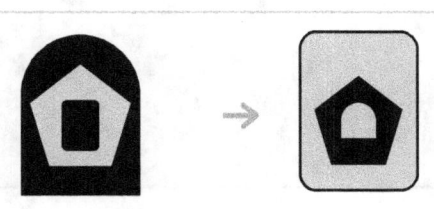

 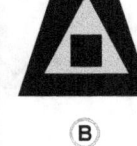 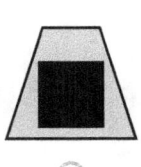  

Ⓐ   Ⓑ   Ⓒ   Ⓓ   Ⓔ

39

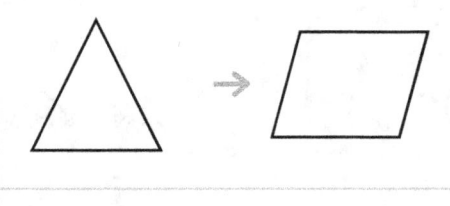

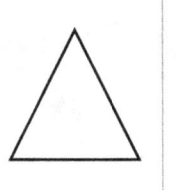 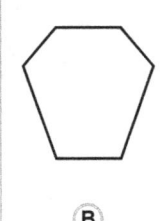 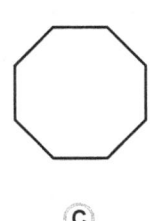 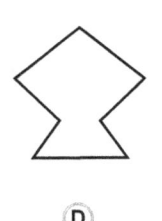 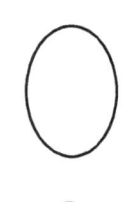

Ⓐ   Ⓑ   Ⓒ   Ⓓ   Ⓔ

FIGURE SERIES

Directions: The pictures inside the boxes go together in a certain way. Another picture should go inside the empty box. Under the boxes is a row of pictures. Which one should go in this empty box?

Tips: See if you can spot the pattern that the design in each box has made, as you go from left to right.

The last box must continue this pattern.

In the example below, there are arrows. They alternate pointing up and pointing down. The quantity in each box forms a pattern: 1 - 2 - 3. After 1 arrow comes 2 arrows. In the last box, there is 1 arrow pointing down. That means that in the next box there must be 2 arrows pointing up.

EXAMPLE

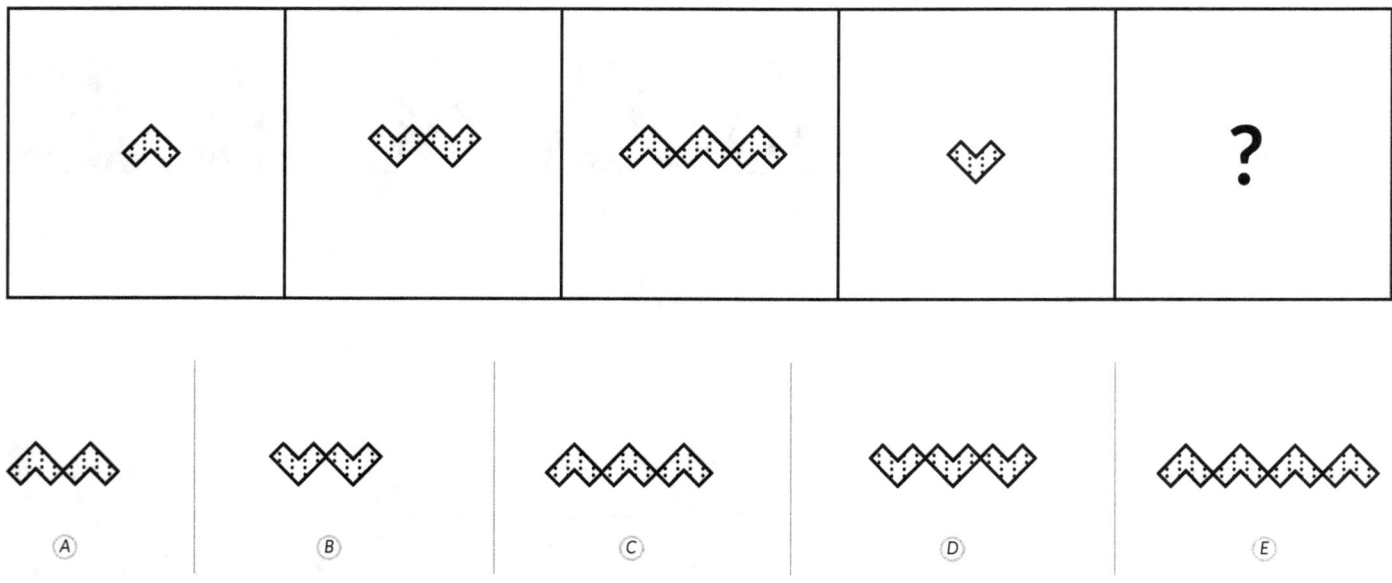

Example Answer: A (See explanations above.)

40

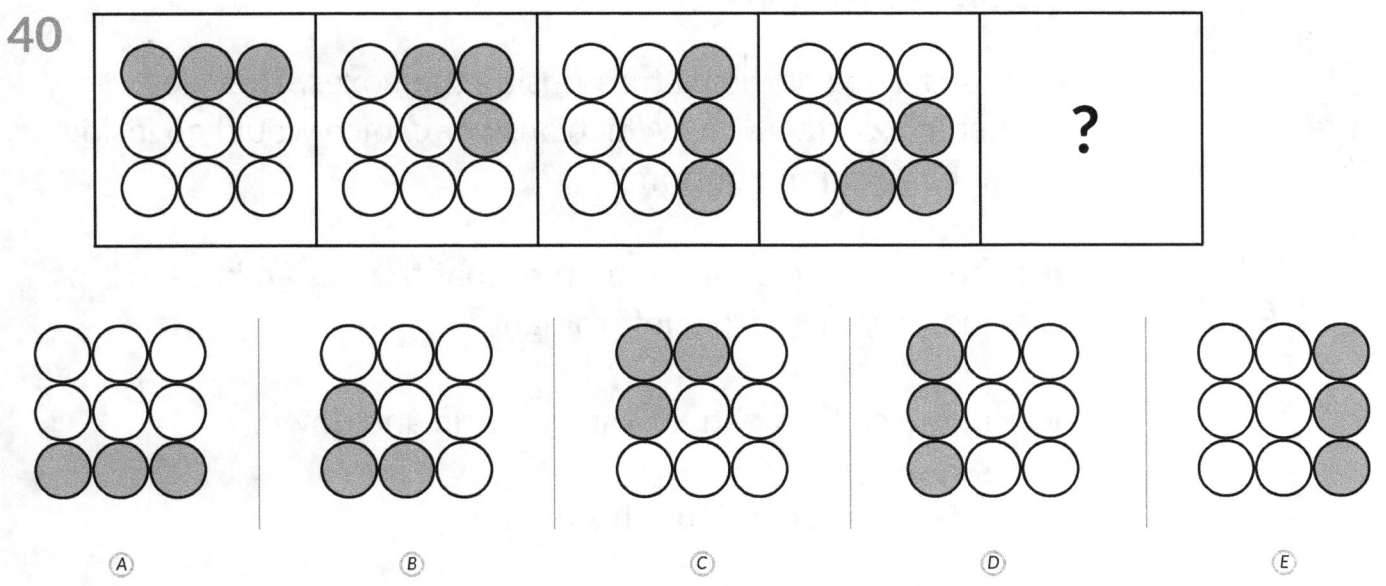

41

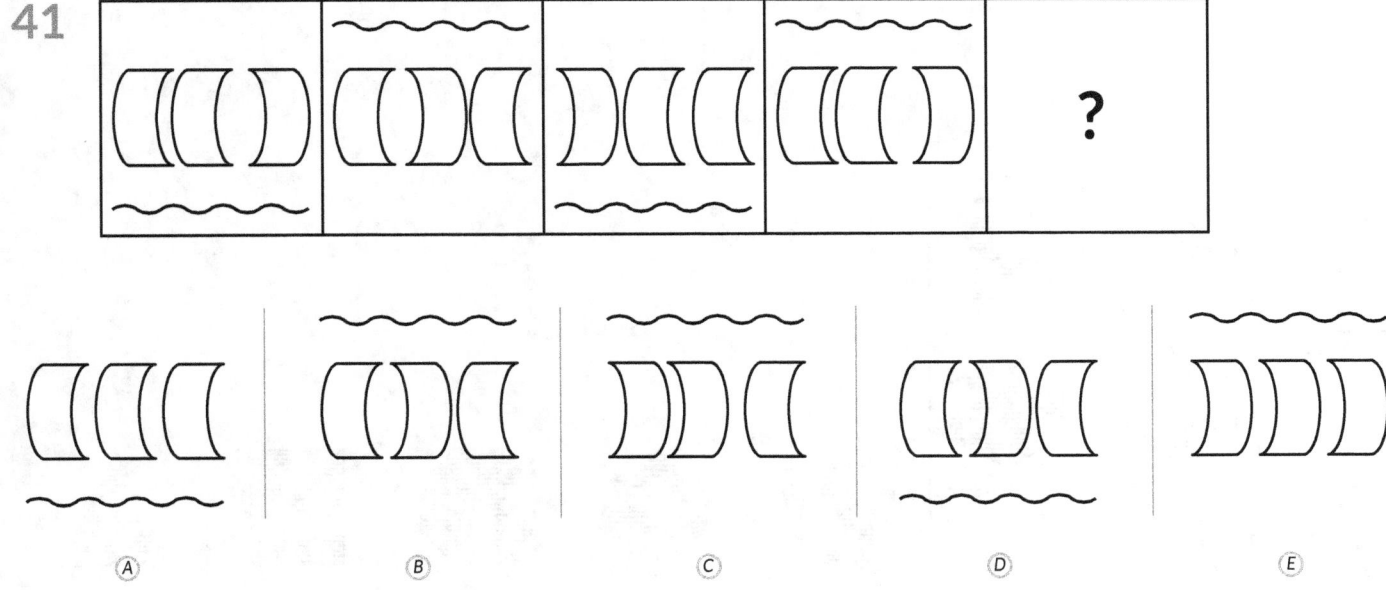

PATTERN MATRIX

Directions: Look at the pictures inside the boxes. They go together in a certain way. Which answer choice would go inside the empty box in the bottom row?

Tips: See if you can spot the pattern that the design in each box has made, as you go from left to right.

There may also be a pattern that goes up and down.

The last box must continue this pattern.

In the example below, going across the first row, we see that there are three different shapes: a four-sided shape, then a 5-sided shape, and finally a six-sided shape. The four-sided shape is white, the 5-sided shape has dots, and the six-sided shape has horizontal lines. Given this, we know that the answer must be a six-sided shape with horizontal lines.

There's also a pattern going down the columns, but it is a different pattern. The first column has a four-sided white shape, the second column has a 5-sided shape filled with dots, and the last column has a 6-sided shape filled with horizontal lines.

EXAMPLE

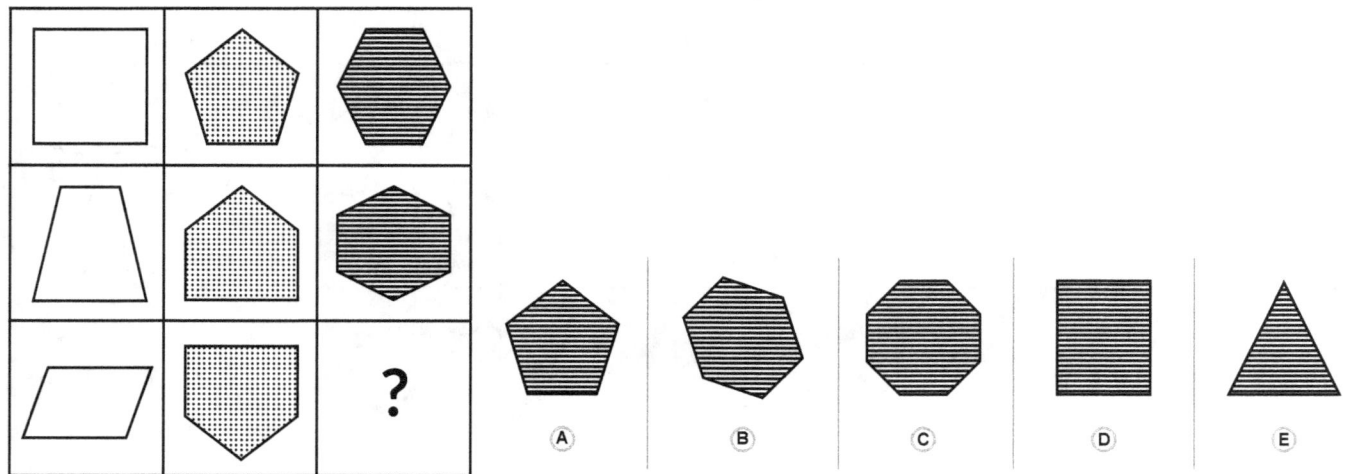

Example Answer: B (See explanation above.)

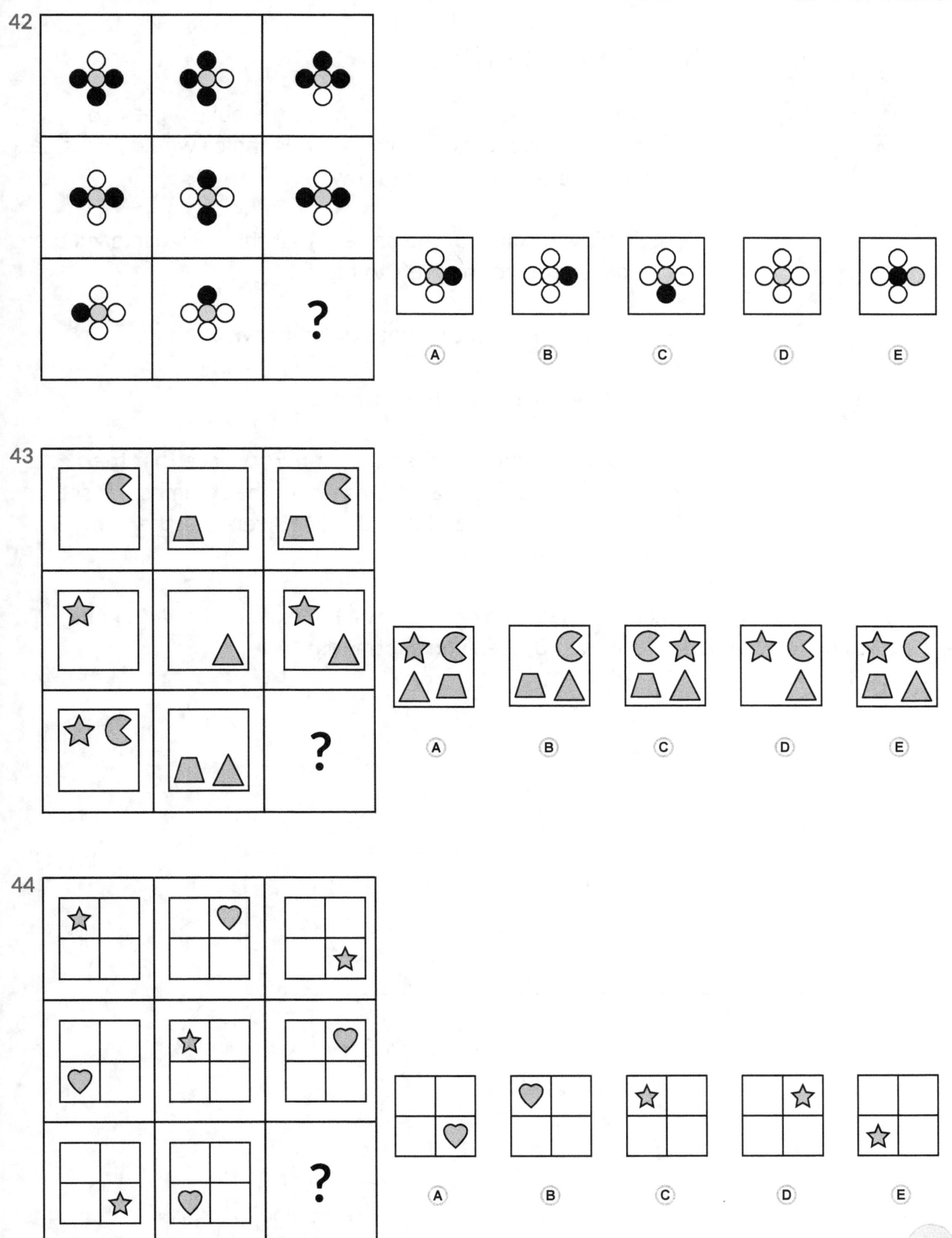

NUMERIC MATRIX

Directions: Look at the numbers inside the boxes. They go together in a certain way. Which answer choice would go inside the empty space in the bottom row?

Tips: See if you can spot the pattern that the design in each box has made, as you go from left to right.

There is also a pattern that goes up and down.

The last row must continue this pattern.

In the example, going across the first row, we see that the pattern is "add 5": 12 + 5 = 17 and 17 + 5 = 22. Going down the columns, we see that the pattern is "subtract 8": 17 - 8 = 9 and 22 - 8 = 14. Given this, the number that goes in place of the question mark is 4.

Note: The pattern may change as you go across rows. For example, in #47, going across the rows, you first subtract 3, then you subtract 5:
32 - 3 = 29, then 29 - 5 = 24.

EXAMPLE

12	17	22
?	9	14

Ⓐ 4   Ⓑ 5   Ⓒ 6   Ⓓ 8   Ⓔ 9

Example Answer: A (See explanation above.)

45

34	22	10
40	?	16

Ⓐ 12　　　Ⓑ 24　　　Ⓒ 28　　　Ⓓ 16　　　Ⓔ 19

46

6	23	30
?	18	25

Ⓐ 1　　　Ⓑ 2　　　Ⓒ 8　　　Ⓓ 6　　　Ⓔ 9

47

32	29	24
28	25	20
26	23	?

Ⓐ 11　　　Ⓑ 23　　　Ⓒ 19　　　Ⓓ 18　　　Ⓔ 29

48

40	45	54
?	51	60
43	48	57

Ⓐ 37　　　Ⓑ 43　　　Ⓒ 45　　　Ⓓ 46　　　Ⓔ 79

NUMERIC INFERENCES

Directions: Look at the first two sets of numbers. The numbers in each set belong together in a certain way. Look at the last set. A number is missing. Which answer choice would go with the number(s) in the last set in the same way that the first two sets go together?

Tips: Use the same methodology to complete Numeric Inferences as you used for Figure Analogies and Verbal Analogies.

Work through these together so your test-taker sees how the first two sets are related.

Together, come up with a "rule" to describe how they are related. Take this "rule," use it together with the missing number in the last set, and figure out which of the answer choices would follow that same rule.

In the example, look at the first set. How would you go from 12 to 18? Try to come up with a rule. You could try the rule "add 6." Now let's check if you can go from 18 to 24 using this rule. (Yes.) This rule must also work for the second group of numbers: 20 + 6 = 26 and 26 + 6 = 32. Finally, 45 + 6 = 51 and 51 + 6 = 57.

Note: The rule can also involve two operations. For example, in #50, in each group of 3 numbers, the first number is added to 9. Then the result is subtracted from 6.

EXAMPLE

[12, 18, 24]   [20, 26, 32]   [45, 51, ?]

Ⓐ 53   Ⓑ 57   Ⓒ 60   Ⓓ 48   Ⓔ 56

Example Answer: B (See explanation above.)

49   [412, 637]   [50, 275]   [99, ?]

Ⓐ 323   Ⓑ 110   Ⓒ 355   Ⓓ 400   Ⓔ 324

50   [9, 18, 12]   [12, 21, 15]   [44, 53, ?]

Ⓐ 11   Ⓑ 40   Ⓒ 55   Ⓓ 47   Ⓔ 49

51   [650, 5]   [491, 9]   [328, ?]

Ⓐ 3   Ⓑ 5   Ⓒ 8   Ⓓ 1   Ⓔ 2

52   [77, 98, 88]   [42, 63, 53]   [12, 33, ?]

Ⓐ 11   Ⓑ 22   Ⓒ 33   Ⓓ 17   Ⓔ 23

NUMERIC SERIES

Directions: Which answer choice would complete the pattern?

Tips: Here, you must figure out a pattern that the numbers have made.

It could involve adding, subtracting, multiplying, or dividing. It could change from one number to the next.

In between each set of numbers, try to figure out what has changed and write it in between the two numbers.

Look at the example below.

How would you go from 89 to 80? You would subtract 9. How would you go from 80 to 71? You would also subtract 9. Let's see if this pattern continues. Going from 71 to 62, then from 62 to 53, and finally from 53 to 44, we see that it does. The pattern is "subtract 9."

Note: Some questions may have a pattern that appears to "skip" numbers. For example, #55, you see that every other number is 9. What pattern can you see that the other numbers have made (the 25, 30, 35 etc.)?

EXAMPLE

| 89 | 80 | 71 | 62 | 53 | 44 | ? |

Ⓐ 35   Ⓑ 34   Ⓒ 39   Ⓓ 9   Ⓔ 29

Example Answer: A (See explanation above.)

53   **31**   **30**   **28**   **27**   **25**   **24**   **22**   **?**

Ⓐ 18   Ⓑ 19   Ⓒ 23   Ⓓ 21   Ⓔ 20

54   **20**   **21**   **22**   **24**   **25**   **26**   **28**   **?**

Ⓐ 31   Ⓑ 32   Ⓒ 30   Ⓓ 27   Ⓔ 29

55   **9**   **25**   **9**   **30**   **9**   **35**   **9**   **?**

Ⓐ 14   Ⓑ 9   Ⓒ 40   Ⓓ 45   Ⓔ 5

56   **20**   **9**   **21**   **10**   **22**   **11**   **23**   **12**   **24**   **?**

Ⓐ 25   Ⓑ 15   Ⓒ 13   Ⓓ 14   Ⓔ 22

- Practice Test 2 Begins On The Next Page -

*Note: Questions in Practice Test 2 & 3 are <u>not</u> grouped by question type (unlike Practice Test 1). When your student takes the actual test, questions will most likely not be grouped by question type.

PRACTICE TEST 2

1 **The opposite of instant is _____.**

  Ⓐ direct   Ⓑ gradual   Ⓒ rapid   Ⓓ immediate Ⓔ circular

---

2 **The words below must be arranged to make the best sentence. Which letter would the <u>last</u> word of the sentence begin with? Here are the words:**

  kind friendships build strong helps being to others

  Ⓐ K   Ⓑ F   Ⓒ B   Ⓓ S   Ⓔ H

---

3 **Samantha and Jake played a game of soccer against Olivia and Mark. During the game, Samantha scored 10 goals, Jake scored 12, Olivia scored 8, and Mark scored 9. How many goals did Samantha and Jake's team score in all?**

  Ⓐ 18   Ⓑ 22   Ⓒ 20   Ⓓ 25   Ⓔ 21

---

4 **Which choice makes the second set of pictures go together in the same way as the first set?**

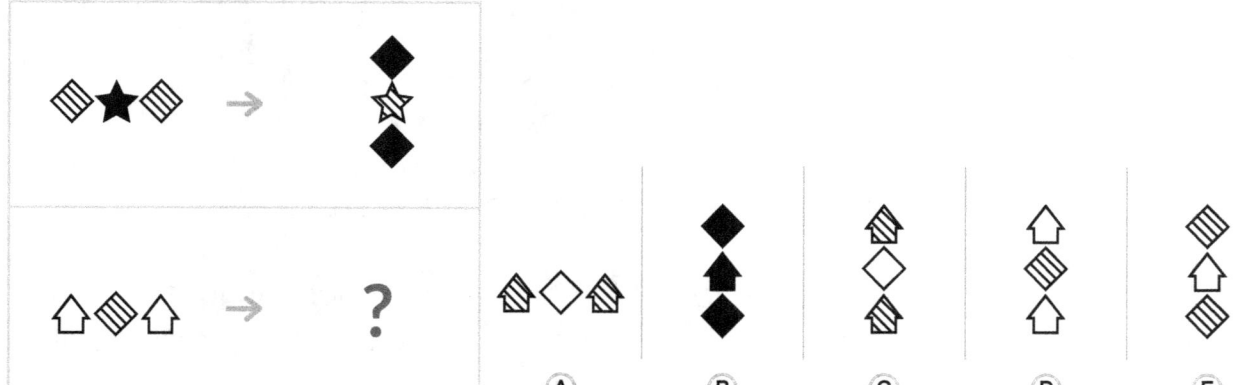

5   **The opposite of ascend is _____.**

(A) extend   (B) increase   (C) remain   (D) assist   (E) descend

6   **A library must always have _____.**

(A) chairs   (B) books   (C) computers   (D) desks   (E) a quiet area

7   **Which word does not go with the others?**

(A) basement   (B) vault   (C) cavern   (D) mountain   (E) cellar

8   **Which word does not go with the others?**

(A) opponent   (B) competitor   (C) rival   (D) challenger   (E) umpire

9   **Julia has fewer apples than Kate. Lucas has more apples than Mike, but fewer than Julia. Which one is not true?**

(A) Kate has the most apples.

(B) Julia has more apples than Mike.

(C) Lucas has more apples than Mike.

(D) Kate has more apples than Lucas.

(E) Julia has the fewest apples.

10 The words below need to be arranged to make the best sentence. Which letter would the <u>last</u> word of the sentence begin with? Here are the words:

truth   telling   trust   the   builds   your   with   friends

(A) T   (B) B   (C) Y   (D) W   (E) F

---

11 Lily had 12 marbles, and she gave 5 of them to Tom. The rest she gave to Alex. Alex then gave 2 marbles to Tom. How many marbles were given to Tom?

(A) 5   (B) 7   (C) 8   (D) 9   (E) 10

---

12 Which choice makes the second set of pictures go together in the same way as the first set?

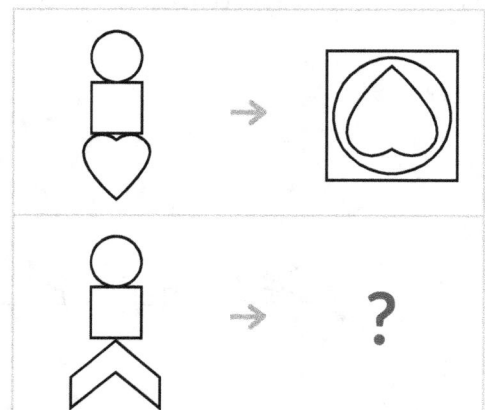

(A)   (B)   (C)   (D)   (E)

---

13 The numbers in the below box go together in a certain way. Which answer choice would replace the question mark?

18	9	13
22	11	15
26	?	17

(A) 12   (B) 13   (C) 15   (D) 6   (E) 22

14 Which answer choice best completes the sentence?

After weeks of _____, the two enemies finally ended the conflict.

Ⓐ agreement   Ⓑ cooperation   Ⓒ unity   Ⓓ satisfaction   Ⓔ disagreement

---

15

cl	ck	clock
bl	ck	?

Ⓐ block   Ⓑ black   Ⓒ bleak   Ⓓ blink   Ⓔ brick

---

16 The opposite of essential is _____.

Ⓐ unstable   Ⓑ unnecessary   Ⓒ relevant   Ⓓ vital   Ⓔ colorful

---

17 Which answer choice best completes the sentence?

One hundred years is the _____ of one century.

Ⓐ greater   Ⓑ equivalent   Ⓒ lesser   Ⓓ half   Ⓔ opposite

---

18 What number should replace the question mark (?) so that all three sets of numbers go together in the same way?

[546, 501, 480]   [790, 745, 724]   [285, ?, 219]

Ⓐ 245   Ⓑ 298   Ⓒ 240   Ⓓ 877   Ⓔ 264

19 The words below must be arranged to make the best sentence. Which letter would the <u>first</u> word of the sentence begin with? Here are the words:

mistakes   from   learning   helps   improve   you

Ⓐ M   Ⓑ F   Ⓒ L   Ⓓ I   Ⓔ Y

20 Ben has twenty-five apples. He gave all but five to Chloe. How many apples does Ben have now?

Ⓐ 5   Ⓑ 10   Ⓒ 15   Ⓓ 20   Ⓔ 25

21 A house must always have _____.

Ⓐ windows   Ⓑ lights   Ⓒ walls   Ⓓ electricity   Ⓔ a kitchen

22 Which answer choice makes the second set of words go together in the same way that the first set does?

sundial → clock : abacus → ?

Ⓐ beads   Ⓑ calculator   Ⓒ measuring tape   Ⓓ addition   Ⓔ compass

23 Which answer choice makes the second set of words go together in the same way that the first set does?

peach → pit : Earth → ?

Ⓐ continent   Ⓑ planet   Ⓒ crust   Ⓓ core   Ⓔ magma

24   The words below need to be arranged to make the best sentence. Which letter would the <u>last</u> word of the sentence begin with? Here are the words:

that   care   others   you   about   respecting   shows   them

(A) R   (B) C   (C) O   (D) Y   (E) T

---

25   A train must always have _____.

(A) an engine   (B) passengers   (C) wheels   (D) windows   (E) a driver

---

26   Which answer choice makes the second set of words go together in the same way that the first set does?

silver → gold : helium → ?

(A) fuel   (B) element   (C) jewelry   (D) balloon   (E) oxygen

---

27   Which answer choice makes the second set of words go together in the same way that the first set does?

equal → equivalent : adequate → ?

(A) sufficient   (B) inadequate   (C) aide   (D) appreciate   (E) alike

---

28   The words in the below box go together in a certain way. Which answer choice would go in place of the question mark?

lo	lk	look
go	gd	?

(A) goat   (B) gold   (C) good   (D) cook   (E) gook

29   The opposite of reveal is _____.

(A) conceal   (B) appeal   (C) publish   (D) complicate   (E) strengthen

30   Which answer choice best completes the sentence?

Only a small car can fit into that _____ parking spot.

(A) broad   (B) spacious   (C) ample   (D) expanded   (E) compact

31   Sofia's flight was scheduled to depart at 3:00 PM. She arrived at the airport 30 minutes early. The flight was delayed and did not depart until 3:45 PM. How many minutes did Sofia wait for her flight?

(A) 30   (B) 45   (C) 60   (D) 75   (E) 90

32   A river must have had _____ at some time.

(A) fish   (B) water   (C) plants   (D) rocks   (E) sand

33   The numbers below form a pattern. What number should go in place of the question mark to continue the pattern?

8.4   10.4   12.4   14.4   16.4   ?

(A) 16.6   (B) 20.4   (C) 18.4   (D) 18.6   (E) 22.4

34   The opposite of ancestor is _____.

     Ⓐ grandparent   Ⓑ descendant   Ⓒ relative   Ⓓ elder   Ⓔ family

35   Which answer choice best completes the sentence?

     The toxic liquid _____ the water in the lake.

     Ⓐ cleans   Ⓑ purifies   Ⓒ refines   Ⓓ contaminates   Ⓔ filters

36   Which word does not go with the others?

     Ⓐ piano   Ⓑ drawer   Ⓒ chest   Ⓓ cabinet   Ⓔ box

37   Which word does not go with the others?

     Ⓐ country   Ⓑ continent   Ⓒ town   Ⓓ headquarters   Ⓔ state

38   The numbers below form a pattern. What number should go in place of the question mark to continue the pattern?

     42   41   40   43   42   41   44   43   ?

     Ⓐ 38   Ⓑ 39   Ⓒ 40   Ⓓ 41   Ⓔ 42

39   The numbers below form a pattern. What number should go in place of the question mark to continue the pattern?

     81   81   79   79   77   77   ?

     Ⓐ 76   Ⓑ 75   Ⓒ 77   Ⓓ 73   Ⓔ 70

40 The words in the below box go together in a certain way. Which answer choice would go in place of the question mark?

bright	light	night
flight	right	?

Ⓐ sight Ⓑ cite Ⓒ sent Ⓓ lite Ⓔ sigh

41 Which choice makes the second set of pictures go together in the same way as the first set?

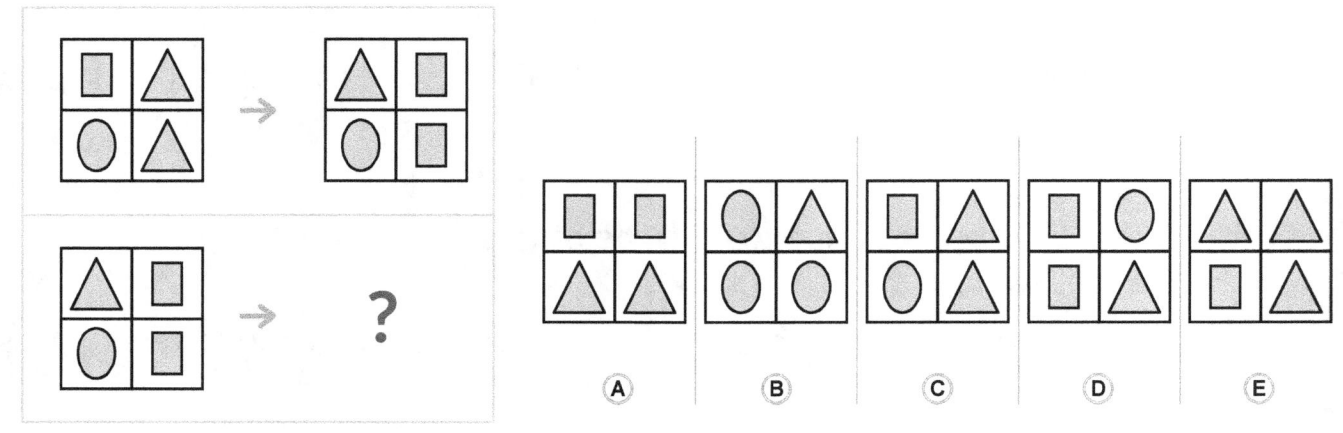

42 Which answer choice makes the second set of words go together in the same way that the first set does?

gum → wrapper : pine → ?

Ⓐ tree Ⓑ bark Ⓒ forest Ⓓ pinecone Ⓔ branch

43 What number comes next in the series?

80   79   77   74   70   65   59   52   ?

Ⓐ 60 Ⓑ 48 Ⓒ 44 Ⓓ 46 Ⓔ 50

44 The words in the below box go together in a certain way. Which answer choice would go in place of the question mark?

letter	crave	strength
later	carve	?

Ⓐ resist   Ⓑ strain   Ⓒ length   Ⓓ train   Ⓔ growth

45 Which choice makes the second set of pictures go together in the same way as the first set?

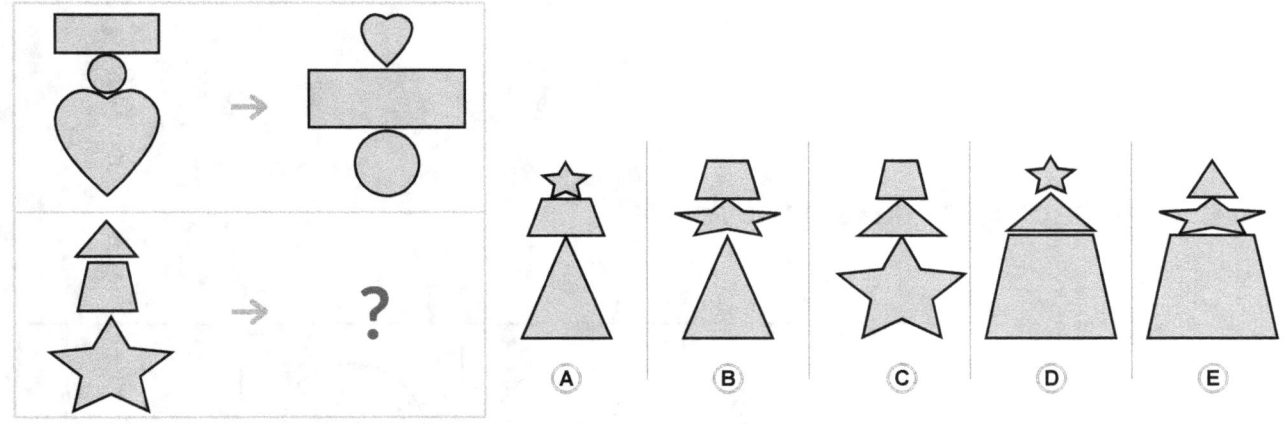

46 What number should replace the question mark (?) so that all three sets of numbers go together in the same way?

[7, 22, 16]   [0, 15, 9]   [?, 30, 24]

Ⓐ 43   Ⓑ 22   Ⓒ 5   Ⓓ 15   Ⓔ 24

47 What number comes next in the series?

49   51   58   57   59   66   65   67   ?

Ⓐ 66   Ⓑ 69   Ⓒ 74   Ⓓ 75   Ⓔ 73

48 The numbers in the below box go together in a certain way. Which answer choice would replace the question mark?

75	?	59
85	74	69
87	76	71

(A) 56 (B) 65 (C) 64 (D) 78 (E) 99

49 What comes next in the series?

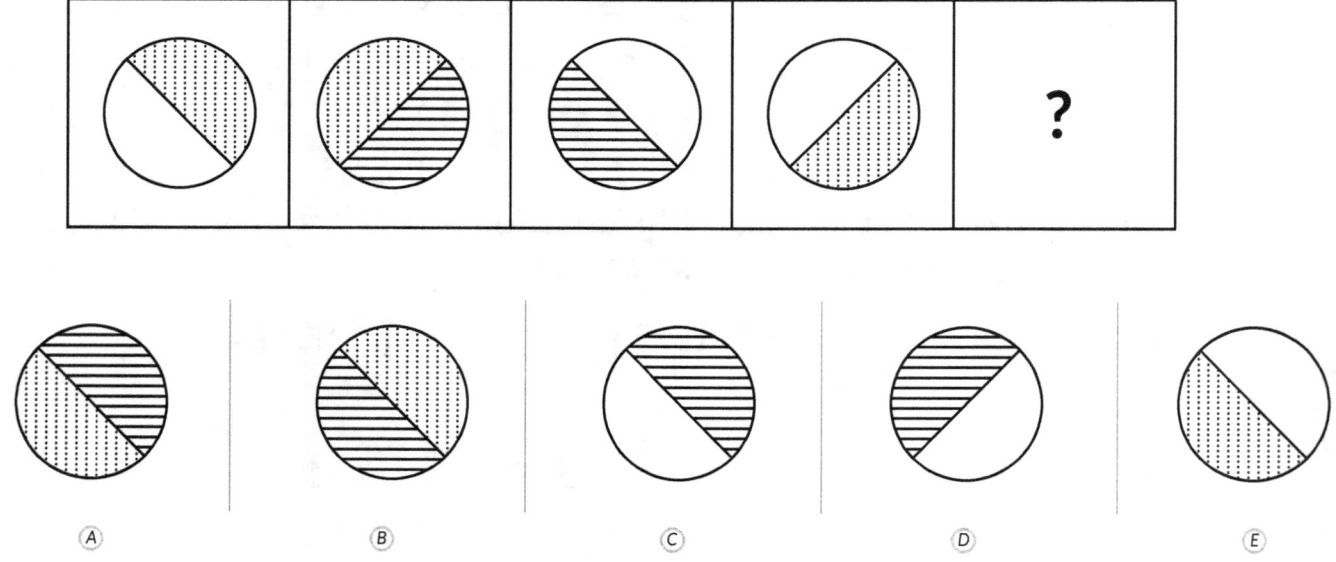

50   The numbers in the below box go together in a certain way. Which answer choice would replace the question mark?

?	13	20
5	10	17
17	22	29

(A) 7   (B) 4   (C) 5   (D) 6   (E) 8

51   What comes next in the series?

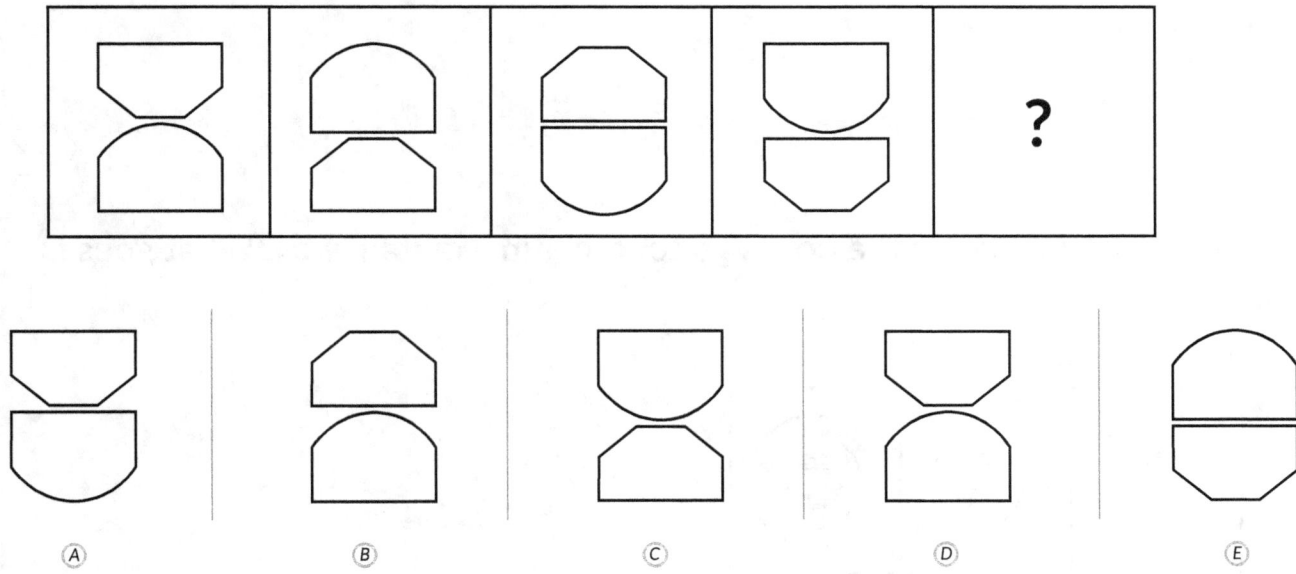

(A)   (B)   (C)   (D)   (E)

52   The numbers in the below box go together in a certain way. Which answer choice would replace the question mark?

1	3	9
4	?	36

(A) 17   (B) 42   (C) 15   (D) 12   (E) 18

53   What comes next in the series?

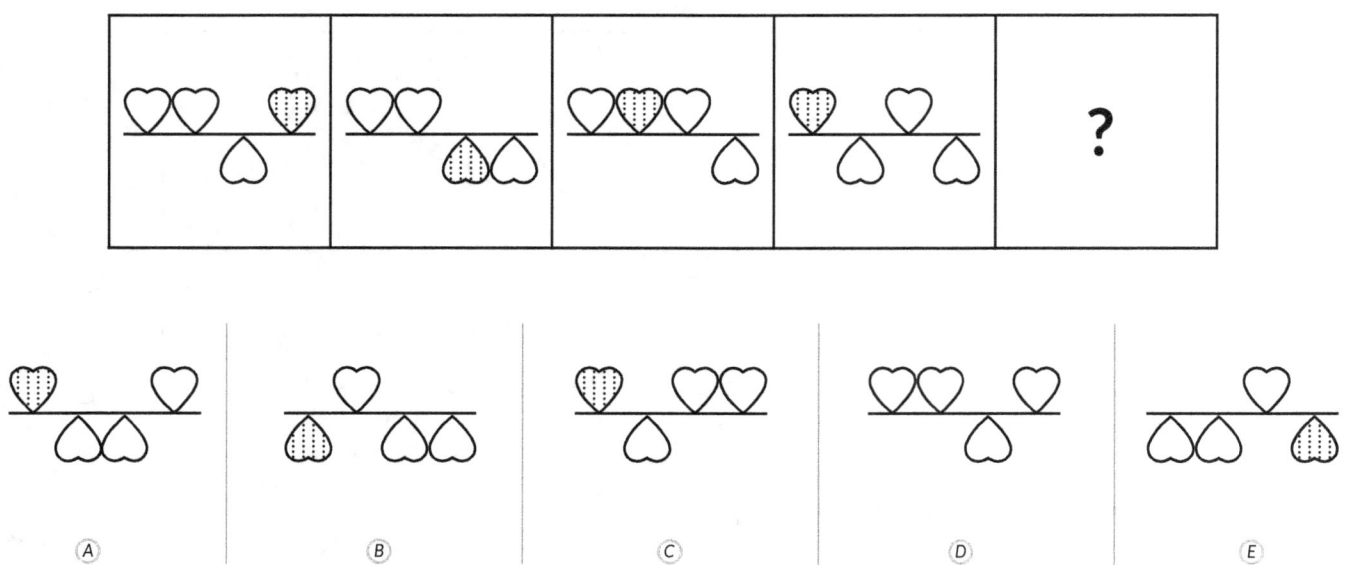

54   The objects in the boxes go together in a certain way. What goes in the empty box?

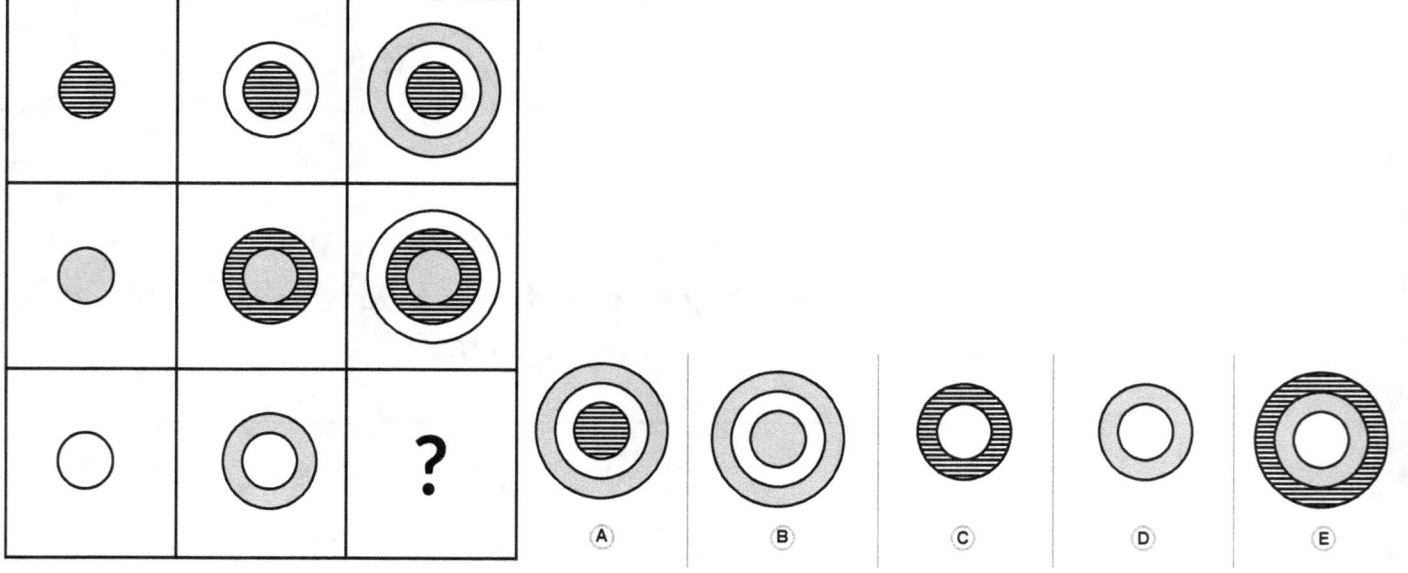

55   What comes next in the series?

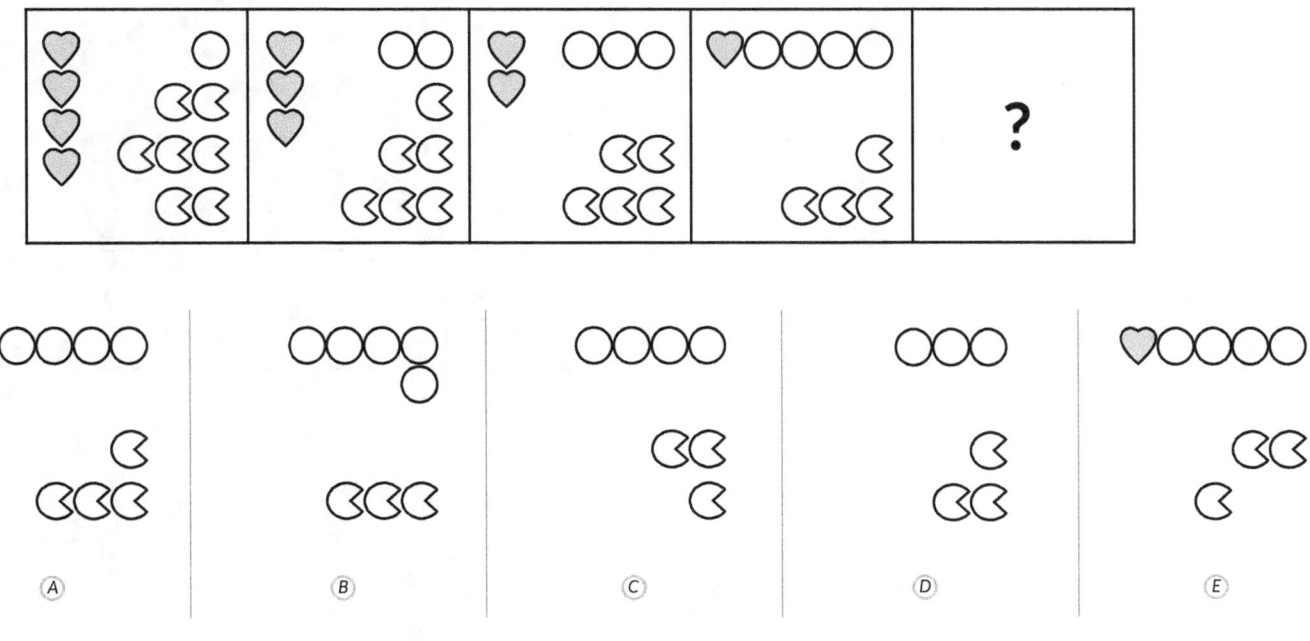

56   The objects in the boxes go together in a certain way. What goes in the empty box?

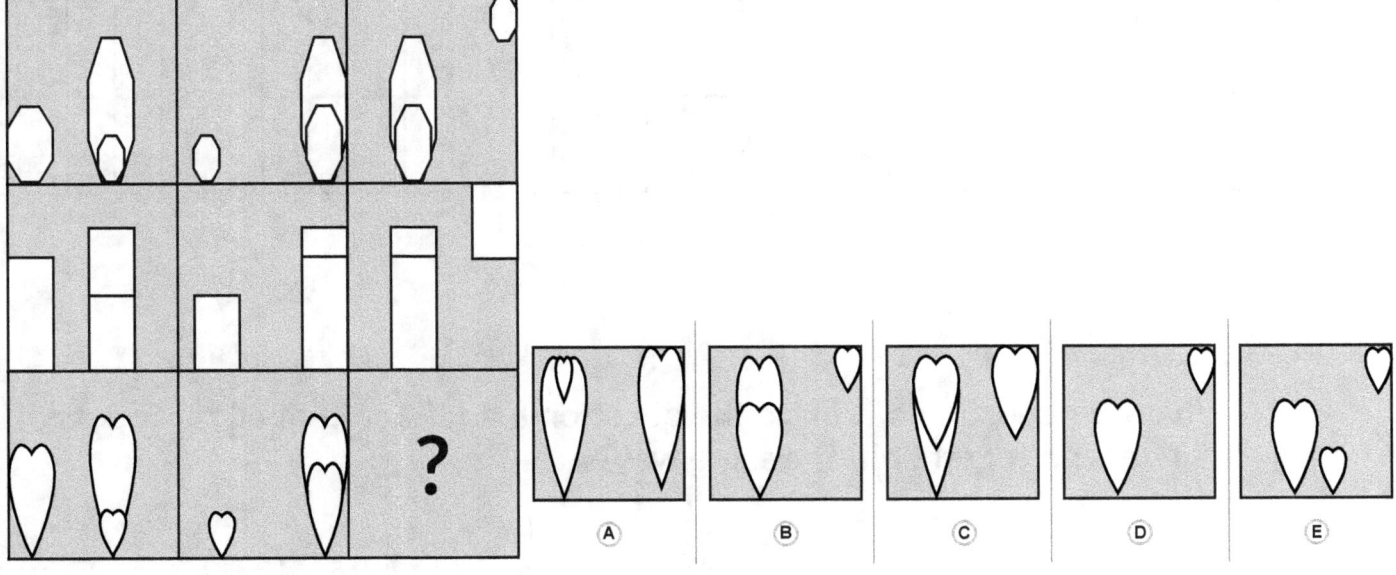

57 The objects in the boxes go together in a certain way. What goes in the empty box?

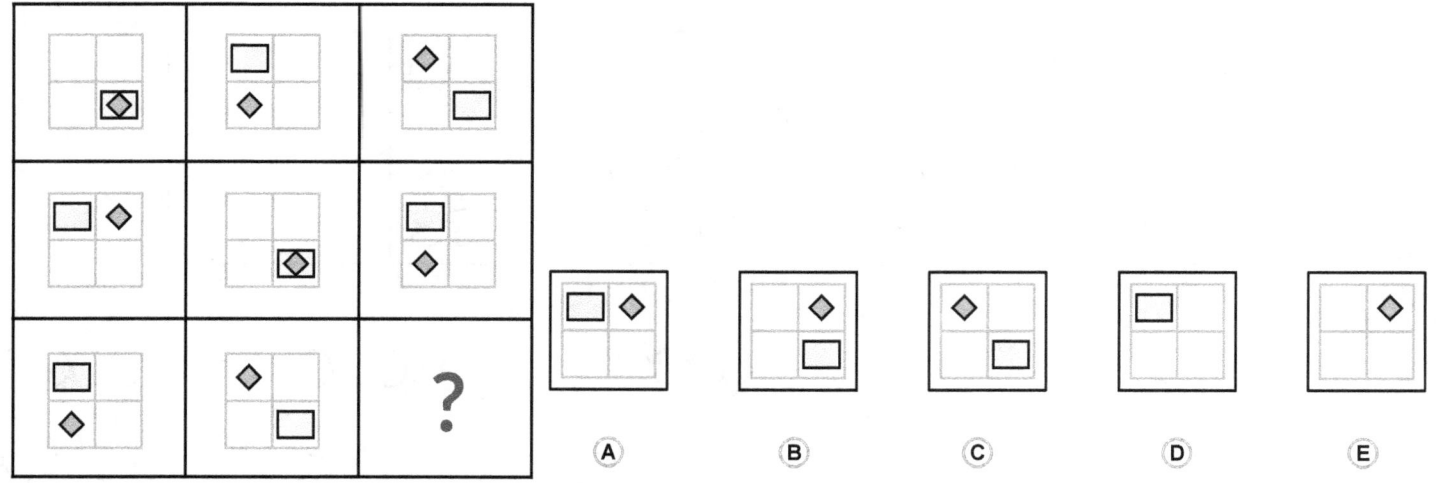

58 What comes next in the series?

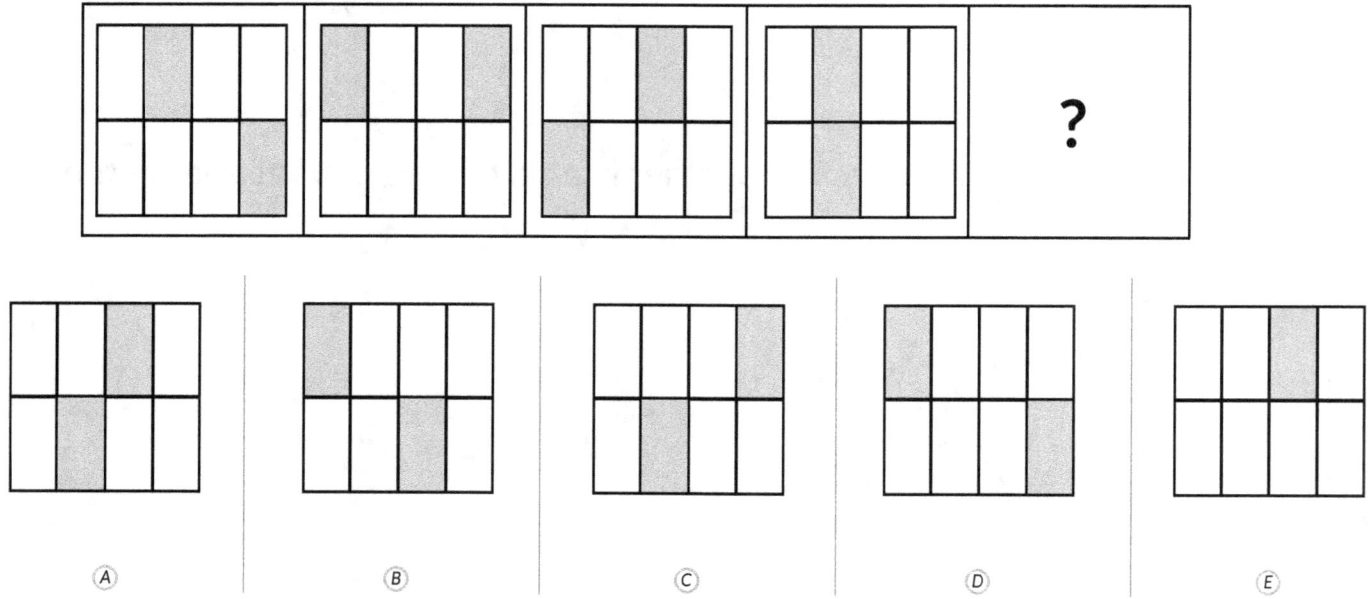

59 What number should replace the question mark (?) so that all three sets of numbers go together in the same way?

[6, 24, 28]   [8, 32, 36]   [?, 44, 48]

Ⓐ 45   Ⓑ 46   Ⓒ 11   Ⓓ 12   Ⓔ 14

60 The objects in the boxes go together in a certain way.
What goes in the empty box?

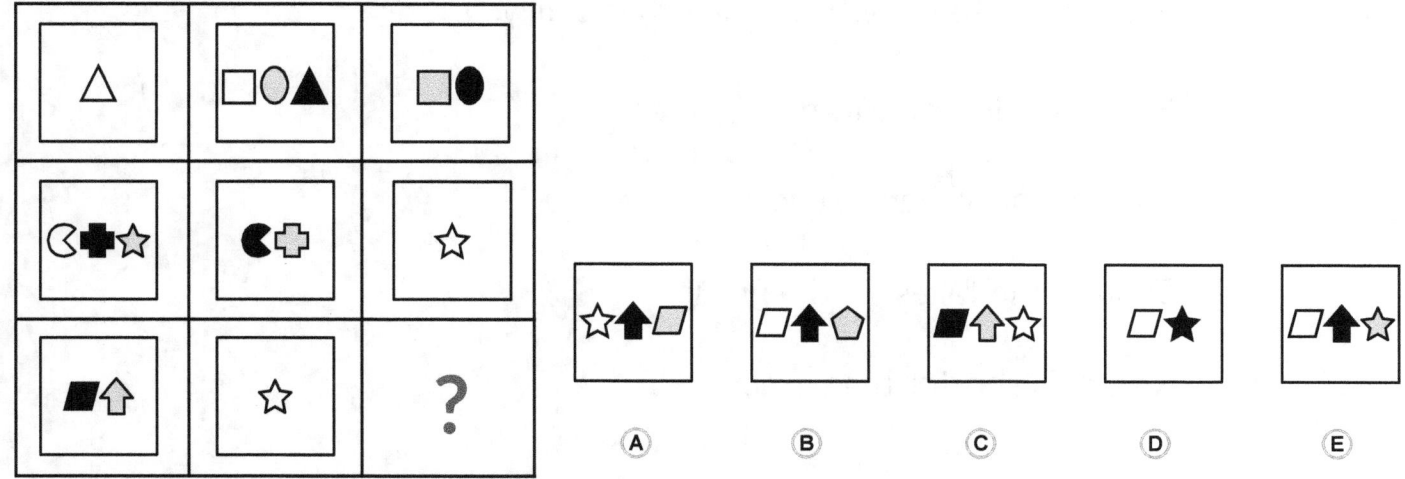

61 The objects in the boxes go together in a certain way. What goes in the empty box?

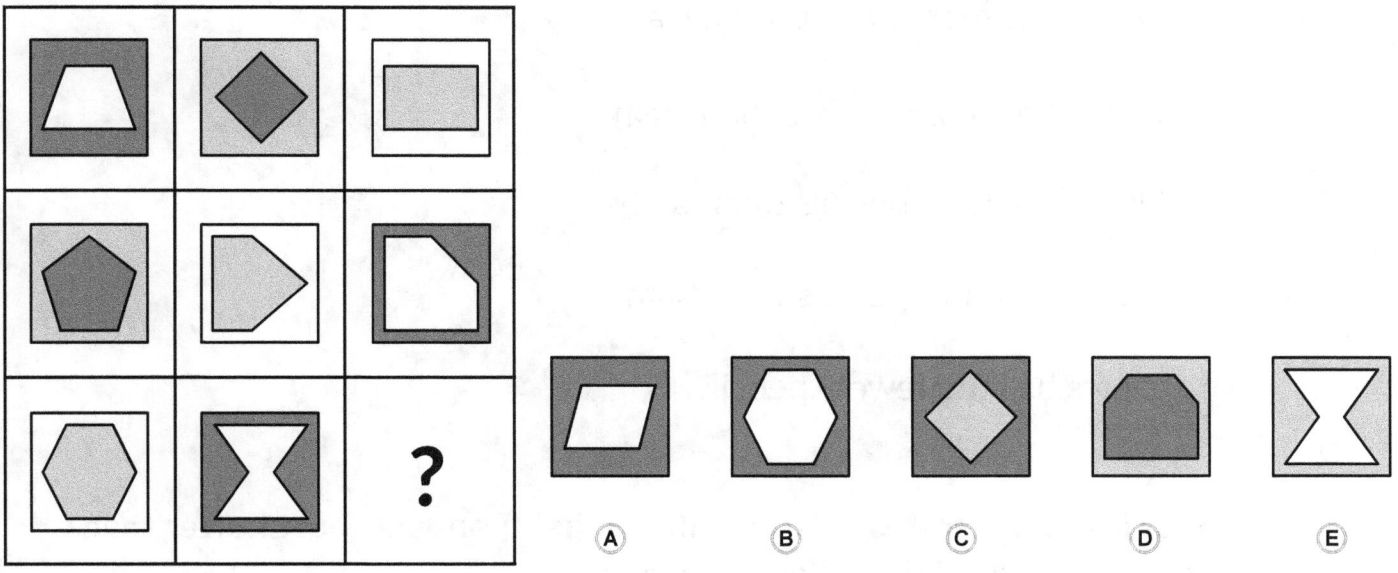

62 What number should replace the question mark (?) so that all three sets of numbers go together in the same way?

[15, 5, 9]   [18, 6, 10]   [?, 4, 8]

Ⓐ 13   Ⓑ 18   Ⓒ 21   Ⓓ 12   Ⓔ 10

63 **Tom is taller than Emily, and Emily is shorter than Rachel. Which of the following do we know for sure is true?**

Ⓐ Rachel and Tom are both taller than Emily.

Ⓑ Emily is taller than Tom.

Ⓒ Emily is taller than Rachel.

Ⓓ Emily is the tallest in the group.

Ⓔ Rachel is shorter than Emily.

64 **Liam has more pencils than Emma. Noah has more pencils than James. Oliver has fewer pencils than Emma but more pencils than James. Which of the following is true?**

Ⓐ Oliver has more pencils than Liam.

Ⓑ Emma has more pencils than Liam.

Ⓒ Noah has more pencils than James.

Ⓓ Noah has more pencils than Liam.

Ⓔ James has the fewest pencils.

65 **Sophia is shorter than Mason. Lily is taller than Jack, but shorter than Sophia. Which of the following is true?**

Ⓐ Sophia is the tallest.

Ⓑ Mason is shorter than Jack.

Ⓒ Lily is shorter than Mason.

Ⓓ Jack is taller than Sophia.

Ⓔ Mason is the same height as Lily.

66 Which answer choice best completes the sentence?

Only an expert jeweler would notice the _____ differences between this real diamond and a fake one.

Ⓐ obvious   Ⓑ clear   Ⓒ noticeable   Ⓓ subtle   Ⓔ expensive

---

67 Which answer choice best completes the sentence?

The two enemies decided to _____ a treaty that both sides would agree to.

Ⓐ negotiate   Ⓑ avoid   Ⓒ refuse   Ⓓ reject   Ⓔ battle

---

68 Which answer choice best completes the sentence?

You can only open and print this document, but if you want to _____ it in any way, you will need the password to make changes.

Ⓐ view   Ⓑ read   Ⓒ notice   Ⓓ modify   Ⓔ skim

---

69 Which answer choice best completes the sentence?

The more _____ a place has, the more homes are required.

Ⓐ tourists   Ⓑ inhabitants   Ⓒ dwellings   Ⓓ vegetation   Ⓔ owners

---

70 What number comes next in the series?

8.4   10.9   13.4   15.9   18.4   ?

Ⓐ 19.5   Ⓑ 19.9   Ⓒ 20.9   Ⓓ 18.9   Ⓔ 23.4

PRACTICE TEST 3

1 The opposite of blossom is _____.

Ⓐ shatter Ⓑ magnify Ⓒ wither Ⓓ scatter Ⓔ develop

2 In a box of crayons, there are twelve crayons. If you bought five boxes, how many crayons would you have in total?

Ⓐ 12 Ⓑ 24 Ⓒ 36 Ⓓ 48 Ⓔ 60

3 What number comes next in the series?

5   20   10   40   20   80   40   ?

○ 40   ○ 80   ○ 60   ○ 100   ○ 160

4 What number should replace the question mark (?) so that all three sets of numbers go together in the same way?

[146, 180, 214]   [118, 152, 186]   [34, 68, ?]

Ⓐ 165 Ⓑ 72 Ⓒ 88 Ⓓ 102 Ⓔ 112

5   The opposite of coax is _____.

Ⓐ encourage   Ⓑ tease   Ⓒ select   Ⓓ force   Ⓔ convince

---

6   On Monday, Lily picked 18 apples from her garden. On Wednesday, she gave away 4 apples to her friend. On Friday, she picked 6 apples and used 5 apples to bake a pie. On Sunday, she picked 7 apples and gave away 3. How many apples does Lily have now?

Ⓐ 19   Ⓑ 22   Ⓒ 25   Ⓓ 24   Ⓔ 18

---

7   Which answer choice makes the second set of words go together in the same way that the first set does?

hoof → giraffe : paw → ?

Ⓐ claw   Ⓑ horse   Ⓒ zebra   Ⓓ rabbit   Ⓔ deer

---

8   What number should replace the question mark (?) so that all three sets of numbers go together in the same way?

[34, 27]   [18, 11]   [27, ?]

Ⓐ 27   Ⓑ 7   Ⓒ 22   Ⓓ 34   Ⓔ 20

9   The opposite of distress is _____.

    Ⓐ consistent   Ⓑ concern   Ⓒ remain   Ⓓ doubt   Ⓔ relief

---

10   Which choice makes the second set of pictures go together in the same way as the first set?

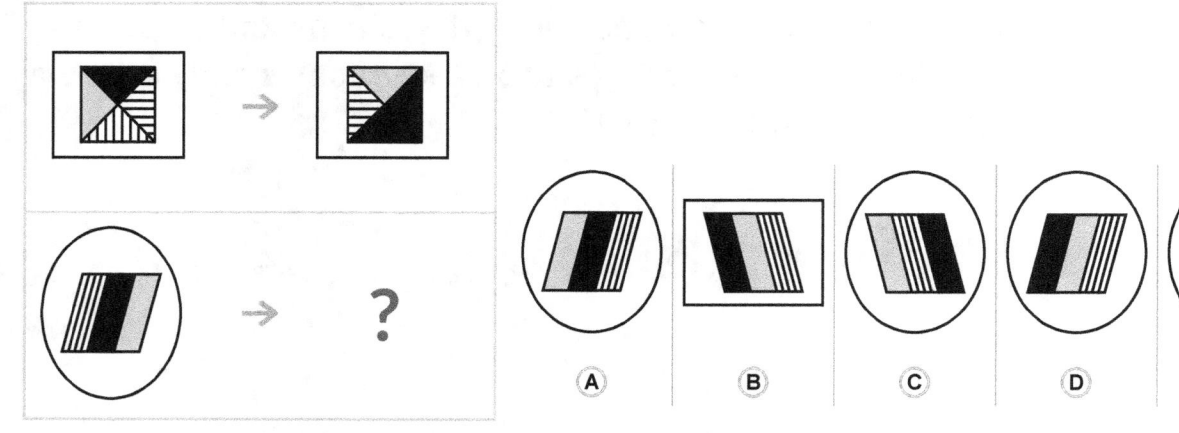

---

11   What number should replace the question mark (?) so that all three sets of numbers go together in the same way?

    [4, 12, 6]   [12, 20, 14]   [22, ?, 24]

    Ⓐ 30   Ⓑ 32   Ⓒ 24   Ⓓ 28   Ⓔ 12

---

12   The numbers in the below box go together in a certain way. Which answer choice would replace the question mark?

43	18	41
79	?	77
62	37	60

    Ⓐ 36   Ⓑ 54   Ⓒ 55   Ⓓ 63   Ⓔ 82

13   The opposite of appropriate is _____.

Ⓐ suitable   Ⓑ complex   Ⓒ improper   Ⓓ fitting   Ⓔ convenient

---

14   Which choice makes the second set of pictures go together in the same way as the first set?

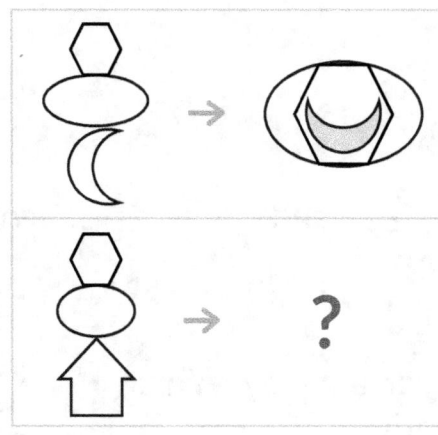

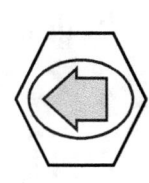   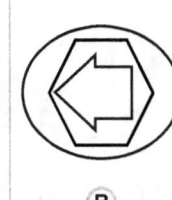   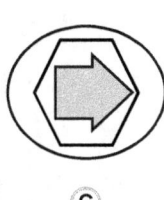      

Ⓐ   Ⓑ   Ⓒ   Ⓓ   Ⓔ

---

15   What number should replace the question mark (?) so that all three sets of numbers go together in the same way?

[5, 30]   [8, 48]   [7, ?]

Ⓐ 70   Ⓑ 42   Ⓒ 47   Ⓓ 34   Ⓔ 13

---

16   What number comes next in the series?

80   72   65   59   54   50   47   45   ?

Ⓐ 40   Ⓑ 46   Ⓒ 42   Ⓓ 43   Ⓔ 44

17 The words below need to be arranged to make the best sentence. Which letter would the <u>first</u> word of the sentence begin with? Here are the words:

someone's   day   kind   brighten   can   words   saying

(A) D   (B) S   (C) K   (D) B   (E) C

---

18 A farm must always have _____.

(A) animals   (B) crops   (C) buildings   (D) land   (E) machinery

---

19 The words in the below box go together in a certain way. Which answer choice would replace the question mark?

te	im	time
et	di	?

(A) tide   (B) dime   (C) emit   (D) edit   (E) mind

---

20 What number should replace the question mark (?) so that all three sets of numbers go together in the same way?

[2, 5]   [7, 15]   [20, ?]

(A) 23   (B) 22   (C) 40   (D) 41   (E) 31

21 The words below need to be arranged to make the best sentence. Which letter would the <u>last</u> word of the sentence begin with? Here are the words:

the started program an the award who recycling student received

(A) A   (B) S   (C) R   (D) T   (E) P

---

22 Which answer choice best completes the sentence?

One of the positive _____ of the Internet is our _____ to access information whenever we need it.

○ connections, need
○ hazards, requirement
○ introductions, barrier
○ ideas, restriction
○ impacts, ability

---

23 A zoo must always have _____.

(A) lions   (B) visitors   (C) animals   (D) a map   (E) cages

---

24 What number should replace the question mark (?) so that all three sets of numbers go together in the same way?

[42, 22]   [58, 30]   [18, ?]

(A) 17   (B) 12   (C) 11   (D) 9   (E) 10

25 The words below need to be arranged to make the best sentence. Which letter would the <u>first</u> word of the sentence begin with? Here are the words:

bakery   took   cupcakes   us   a   bought   to   grandma   we   where

- (A) A
- (B) B
- (C) C
- (D) F
- (E) G

26 Which answer choice best completes the sentence?

People's desire to use less plastic would _____ an increase in the use of plastic _____.

- ○ cause, amounts
- ○ lead to, materials
- ○ result in, alternatives
- ○ merit, bottles
- ○ produce, particles

27 What is seven less than four times five, plus three?

- (A) 10
- (B) 13
- (C) 16
- (D) 18
- (E) 20

28 A mountain must always have _____.

- (A) a peak
- (B) snow
- (C) rocks
- (D) trees
- (E) a canyon

29 The opposite of "simple" is _____.

- (A) easy
- (B) powerful
- (C) massive
- (D) complex
- (E) elegant

30 The words below need to be arranged to make the best sentence. Which letter would the <u>last</u> word of the sentence begin with? Here are the words:

that   wind   have   in   steady   kites   the   strings   keep   them

Ⓐ W   Ⓑ K   Ⓒ S   Ⓓ H   Ⓔ T

---

31 Which answer choice best completes the sentence?

Their new company should be a success - it has the _____ to _____ lots of money.

○ absence, produce   ○ potential, generate   ○ possibility, waste   ○ ability, lose   ○ guarantee, avoid

---

32 What is ten more than three times eight, minus six?

Ⓐ 20   Ⓑ 28   Ⓒ 34   Ⓓ 38   Ⓔ 42

---

33 A mountain must always have _____.

Ⓐ a summit   Ⓑ plants   Ⓒ rocks   Ⓓ animals   Ⓔ boulders

---

34 What number comes next in the series?

51   -50   49   -48   47   -46   45   ?

Ⓐ 44   Ⓑ -44   Ⓒ 43   Ⓓ -43   Ⓔ 46

35 Which answer choice makes the second set of words go together in the same way that the first set does?

foot → sock : planet → ?

Ⓐ Jupiter   Ⓑ sun   Ⓒ rocket   Ⓓ moon   Ⓔ atmosphere

36 Which answer choice makes the second set of words go together in the same way that the first set does?

dim → dark : cool → ?

Ⓐ mild   Ⓑ frigid   Ⓒ chilled   Ⓓ hot   Ⓔ warm

37 Which word does not go with the others?

Ⓐ purse   Ⓑ suitcase   Ⓒ wallet   Ⓓ bookbag   Ⓔ money

38 Which word does not go with the others?

Ⓐ enormous   Ⓑ small   Ⓒ amount   Ⓓ miniature   Ⓔ colossal

39 The words in the below box go together in a certain way. Which answer choice would replace the question mark?

st	am	steam
dr	am	?

Ⓐ drain   Ⓑ dream   Ⓒ seam   Ⓓ draft   Ⓔ drama

40   Which answer choice makes the second set of words go together in the same way that the first set does?

cooperation → partner : competition →   ?

Ⓐ opponent   Ⓑ coach   Ⓒ game   Ⓓ referee   Ⓔ assistant

---

41   Which answer choice makes the second set of words go together in the same way that the first set does?

drought → rain : hunger →   ?

Ⓐ water   Ⓑ thirst   Ⓒ plate   Ⓓ hungry   Ⓔ food

---

42   Which word does not go with the others?

Ⓐ collect   Ⓑ separate   Ⓒ assemble   Ⓓ gather   Ⓔ accumulate

---

43   Which word does not go with the others?

Ⓐ introduction   Ⓑ inauguration   Ⓒ conclusion   Ⓓ birth   Ⓔ dawn

---

44   The words in the below box go together in a certain way. Which answer choice would replace the question mark?

act	inn	end
able	iron	?

Ⓐ edit   Ⓑ enter   Ⓒ eager   Ⓓ enable   Ⓔ exit

45   The words in the below box go together in a certain way. Which answer choice would replace the question mark?

scale	clock	compass
weight	time	?

   Ⓐ date   Ⓑ direction   Ⓒ width   Ⓓ distance   Ⓔ weather

46   Which choice makes the second set of pictures go together in the same way as the first set?

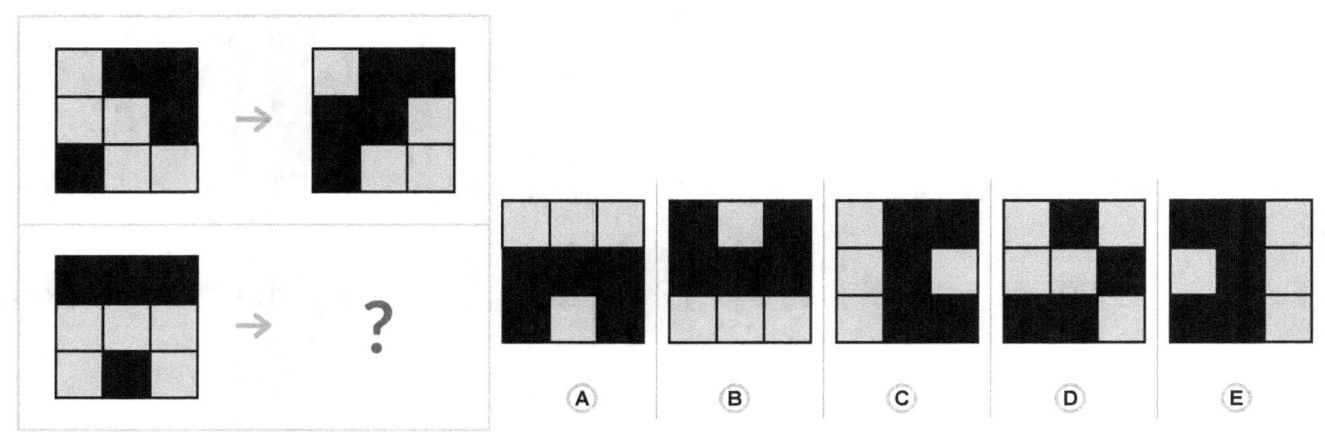

47   Which choice makes the second set of pictures go together in the same way as the first set?

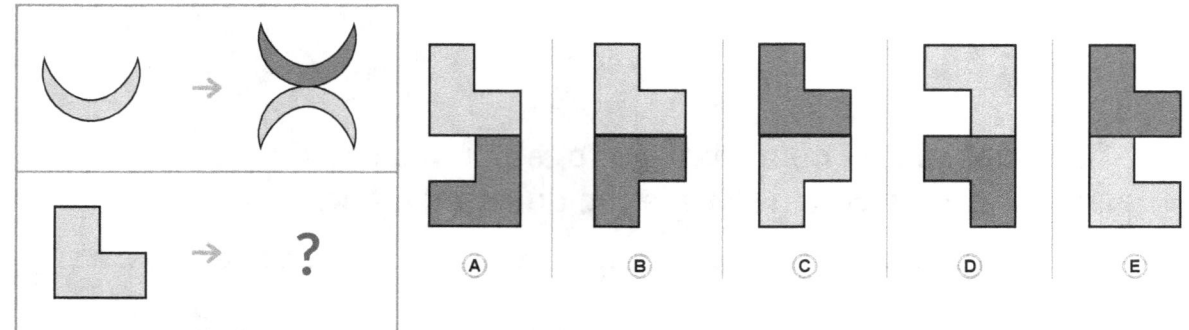

48   What number comes next in the series?

50   49   48   49   46   43   46   42   38   ?

   Ⓐ 38   Ⓑ 46   Ⓒ 45   Ⓓ 42   Ⓔ 44

49   The words in the below box go together in a certain way. Which answer choice would replace the question mark?

mammal	bird	reptile
monkey	bald eagle	?

Ⓐ snail   Ⓑ spider   Ⓒ beetle   Ⓓ lizard

50   Which choice makes the second set of pictures go together in the same way as the first set?

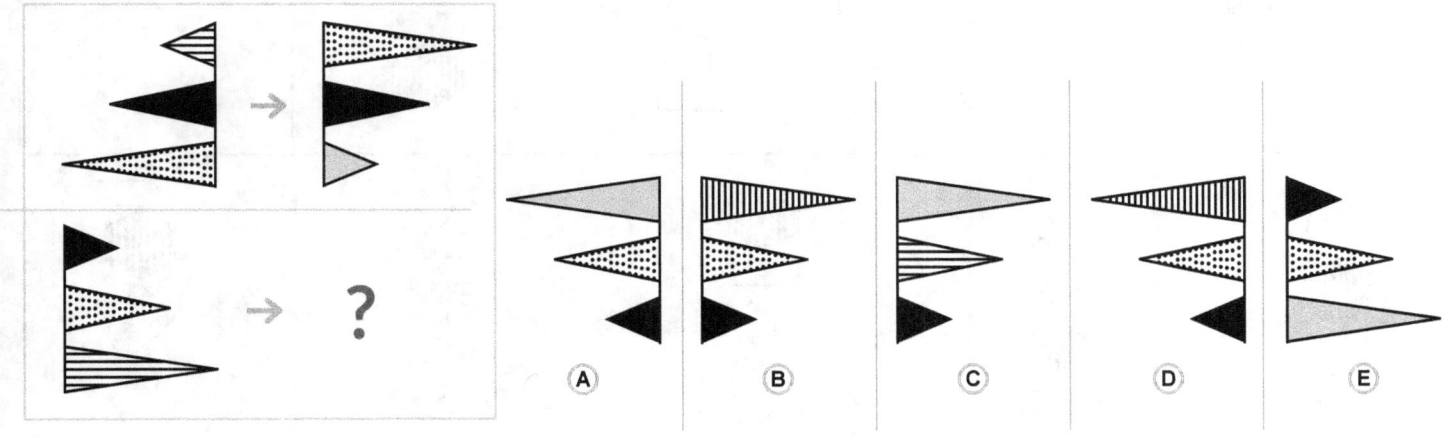

Ⓐ   Ⓑ   Ⓒ   Ⓓ   Ⓔ

51   Which answer choice makes the second set of words go together in the same way that the first set does?

magnify → lens : cut → ?

Ⓐ paper   Ⓑ blade   Ⓒ point   Ⓓ sharpen   Ⓔ carving

52   The numbers in the below box go together in a certain way. Which answer choice would replace the question mark?

62	41	20
53	32	?

Ⓐ 11   Ⓑ 12   Ⓒ 36   Ⓓ 22   Ⓔ 23

---

53   What comes next in the series?

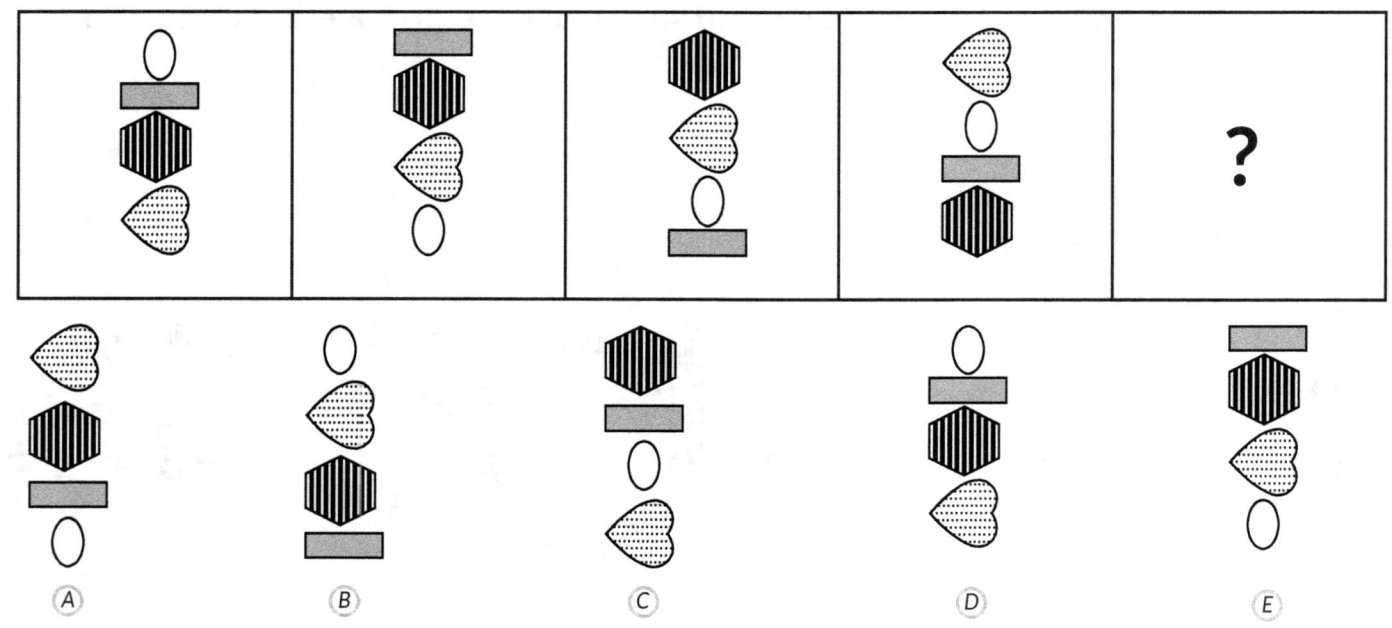

---

54   The numbers in the below box go together in a certain way. Which answer choice would replace the question mark?

36	12	6
12	4	?
24	8	4

Ⓐ 1   Ⓑ 3   Ⓒ 5   Ⓓ 6   Ⓔ 2

55 Which answer choice would replace the question mark?

36	28	32
25	?	21
31	23	27

Ⓐ 45   Ⓑ 21   Ⓒ 23   Ⓓ 17   Ⓔ 40

---

56 The objects in the boxes go together in a certain way.
What goes in the empty box?

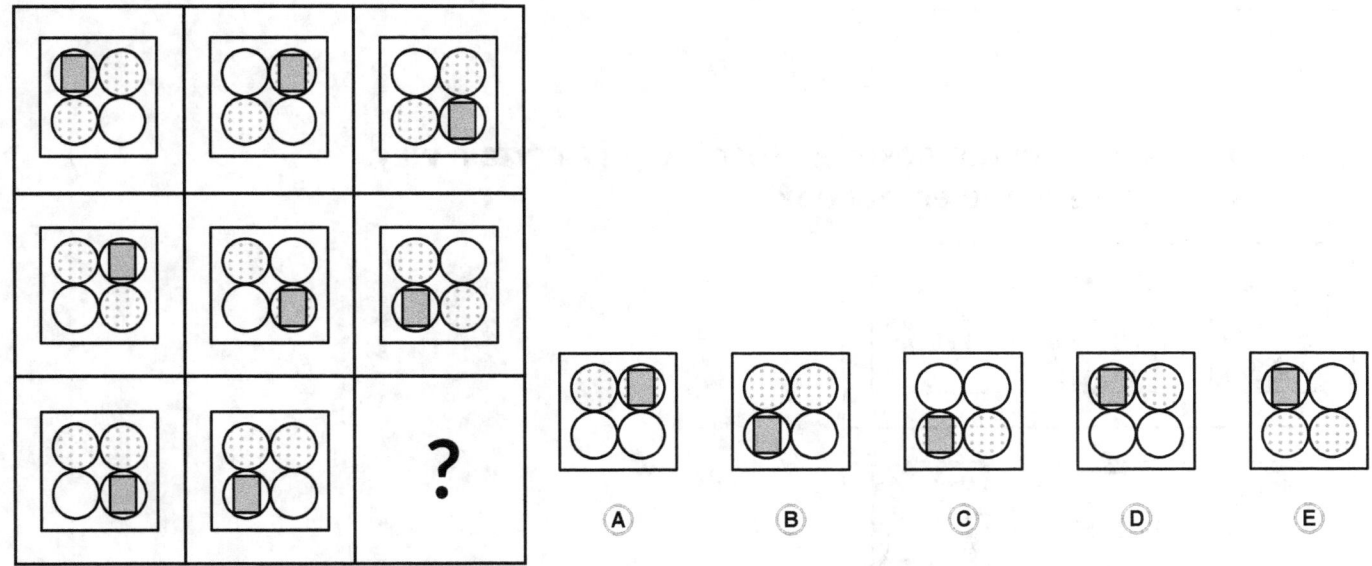

---

57 What comes next in the series?

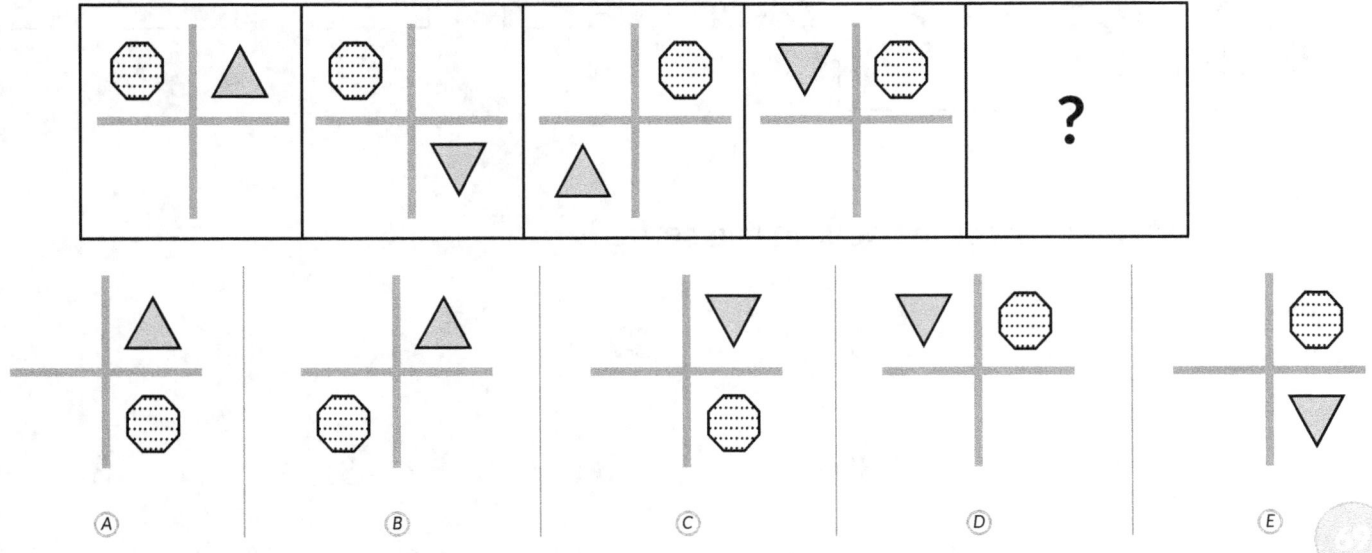

58 The objects in the boxes go together in a certain way.
What goes in the empty box?

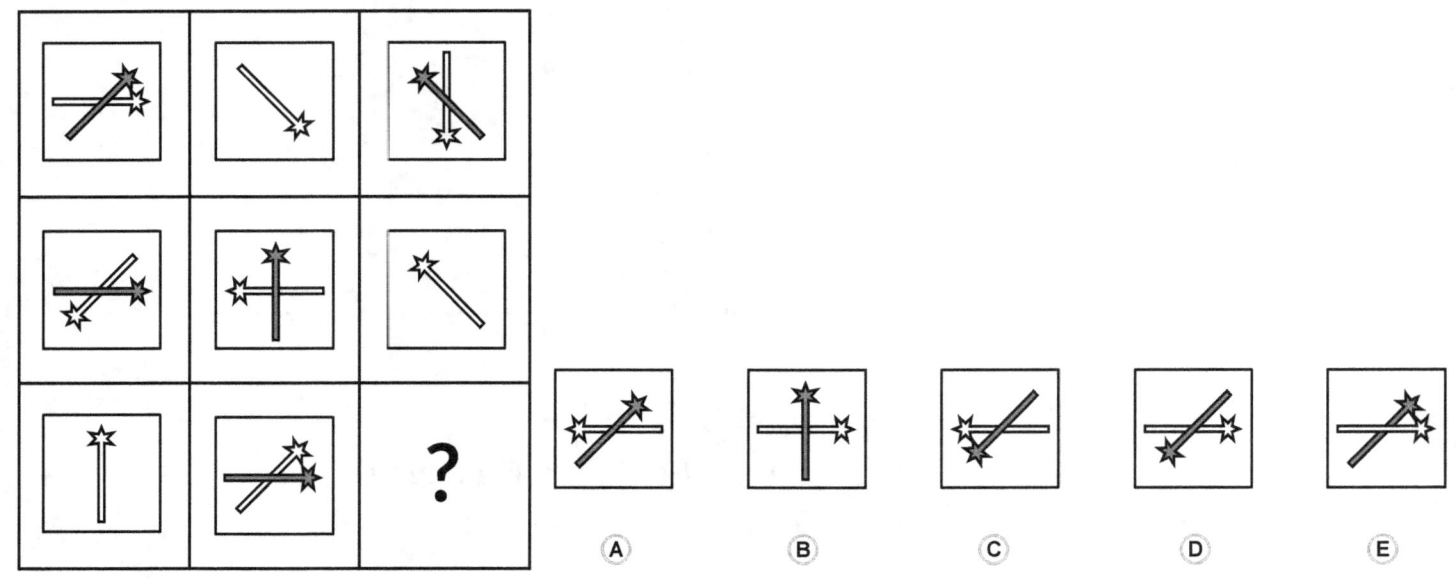

59 The objects in the boxes go together in a certain way.
What goes in the empty box?

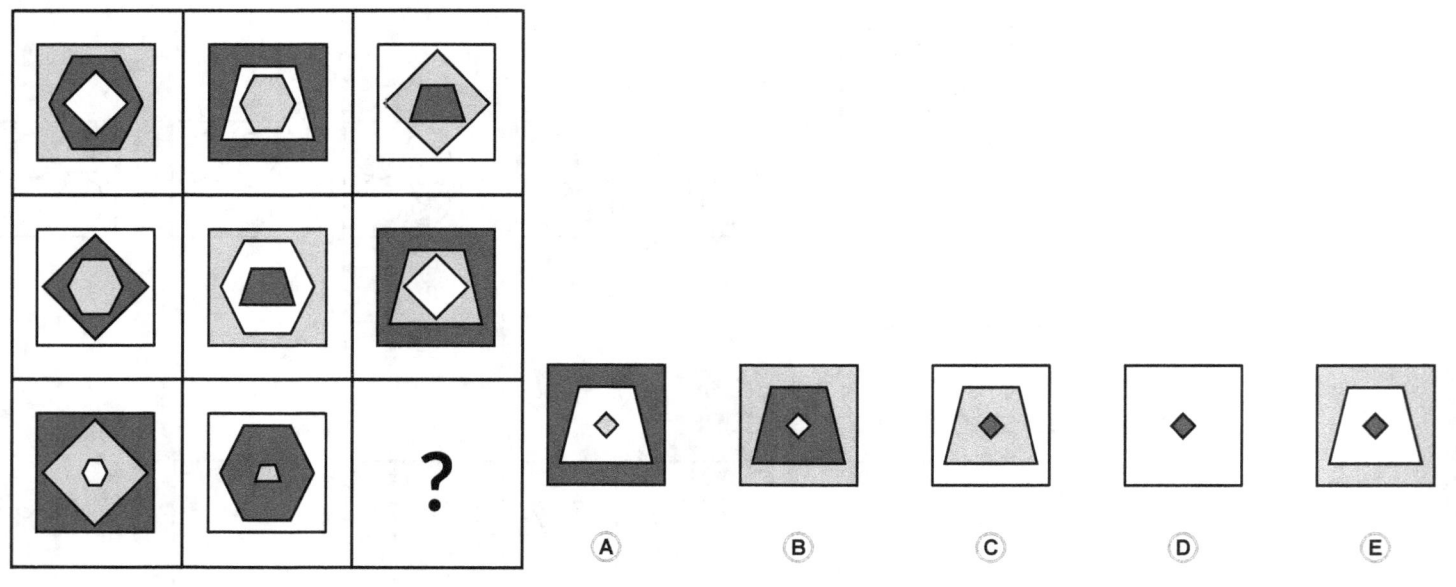

60 What number comes next in the series?

| 1 | 3 | 9 | 27 | ? |

○ 54   ○ 30   ○ 81   ○ 61   ○ 3

61 The objects in the boxes go together in a certain way.
What goes in the empty box?

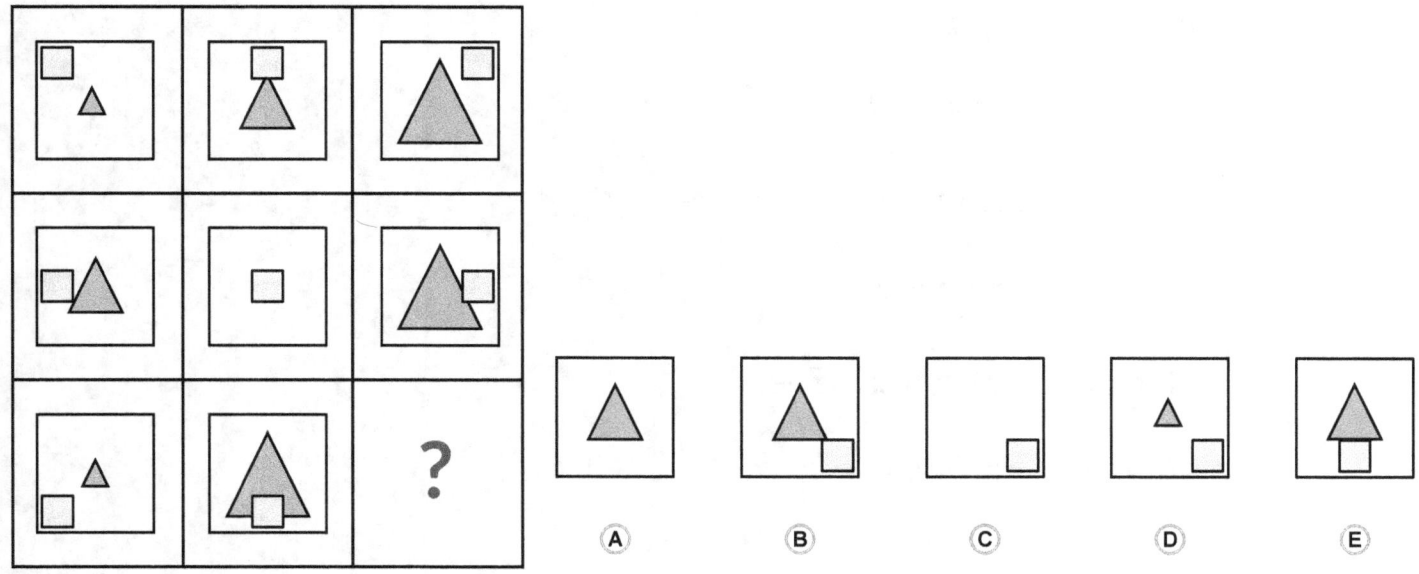

62 What comes next in the series?

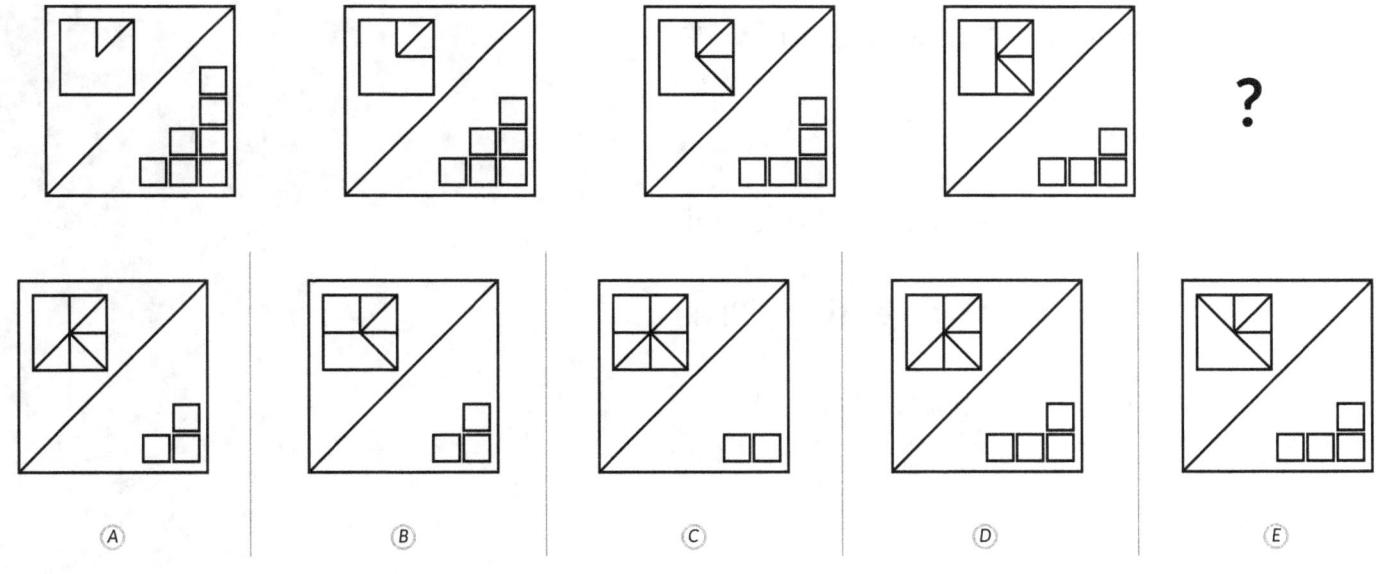

63 What number comes next in the series?

| 2 | 21 | 40 | 59 | 78 | ? |

○ 80   ○ 107   ○ 19   ○ 87   ○ 97

64 James runs faster than Lily. Zoe runs faster than Max but not as fast as Kate. James runs faster than Max but not as fast as Zoe. Which of the following is true?

Ⓐ Zoe runs the slowest.

Ⓑ Lily runs the fastest.

Ⓒ Kate runs the fastest.

Ⓓ Max runs faster than Zoe.

Ⓔ Max runs the slowest.

65 Sarah runs faster than Amy. Amy runs faster than Emma but slower than Olivia. Which of the following <u>must</u> be true?

Ⓐ Emma runs faster than Olivia.

Ⓑ Emma runs the slowest.

Ⓒ Olivia runs slower than Sarah.

Ⓓ Sarah runs slower than Olivia.

Ⓔ Amy runs faster than Sarah.

66 What number comes next in the series?

32   23   31   29   20   28   26   17   25   23   ?

Ⓐ 21   Ⓑ 31   Ⓒ 14   Ⓓ 15   Ⓔ 22

67

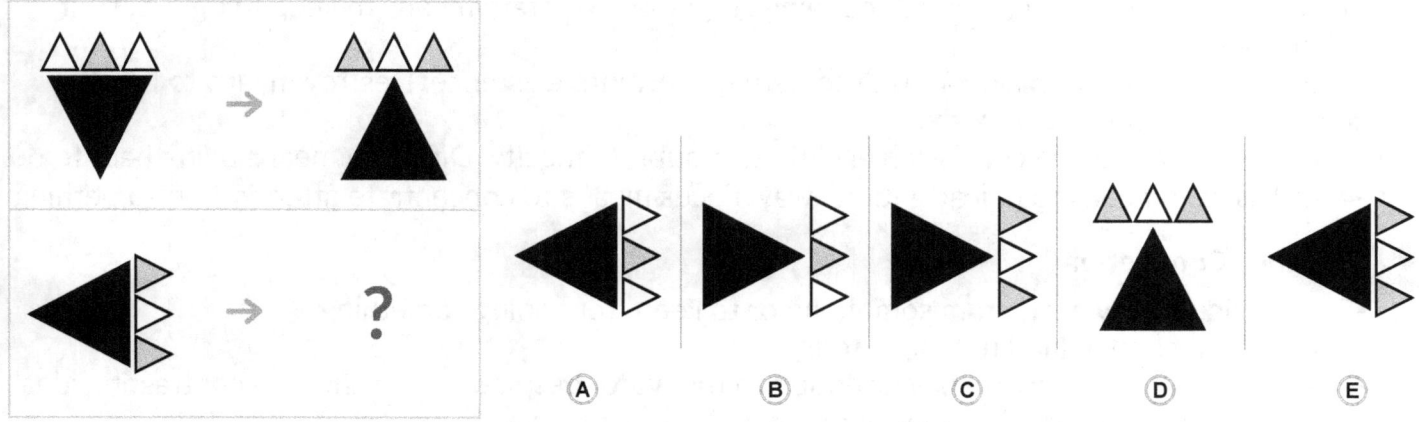

---

68 Which answer choice makes the second set of words go together in the same way that the first set does?

drawer → reward : loots →

Ⓐ tools   Ⓑ stool   Ⓒ tolls   Ⓓ stools   Ⓔ toll

---

69 Which answer choice makes the second set of words go together in the same way that the first set does?

jacket → sleeve : tree →

Ⓐ forest   Ⓑ orchard   Ⓒ oak   Ⓓ bark   Ⓔ branch

---

70 Which answer choice makes the second set of words go together in the same way that the first set does?

social studies → geography : science →

Ⓐ biology   Ⓑ history   Ⓒ biologist   Ⓓ experiment   Ⓔ planetary

- End of Practice Tests -

ANSWER KEY FOR PRACTICE TEST 1 (WORKBOOK FORMAT)

Antonyms

-1. B: Blend means to mix or combine things together. Separate means to keep things apart or divide them.
-2. E: Create means to make or bring something new into existence. Destroy means to break something so it no longer exists.
-3. A: Ease means being comfortable, without trouble/difficulty. Difficulty means being hard to do.
-4. D: Distract means to pull attention away. Focus means to concentrate attention on something.

Sentence Completion

-5. D. avoid: to stay away from something or to keep from doing something
-6. E. abrupt: sudden (and not expected)
-7. A. seldom: not often; also pay attention to the word "despite," which shows a contrasting idea and the word "brief," which means very short
-8. E. capture: to take into your control; notorious: famous for something bad

Sentence Arrangement

-9. D. Sentence: Birds have feathers that help them fly in the air.
-10. D. Sentence: The sun provides heat and light to Earth. (Note that the sentence could also be: The sun provides light and heat to Earth. In both sentences, the first word remains the same.)
-11. B. Sentence: Magnets can attract metals like iron.
-12. B. Sentence: Sharing toys with friends makes everyone happy.

Arithmetic Reasoning

-13. B: 100 + 30 - 25 + 15 - 40 = 80
-14. C: "Eight more than ten times five" means you first calculate "ten times five" and then add 8. Multiply 10 by 5: $10 \times 5 = 50$. Then, add 8: $50 + 8 = 58$.
-15. A: For the first 4 desks, the teacher places 3 books on each desk: $4 \times 3 = 12$ books.
For the remaining 4 desks, the teacher places 5 books on each desk: $4 \times 5 = 20$ books.
Now, add both totals together: 12 + 20 = 32 books.
-16. D: "Five more than three times six, minus four" can be written as: $(3 \times 6) + 5 - 4 = 19$.

Logical Selection

-17. B: A school must have students to be a school. While many schools have cafeterias, libraries, playgrounds, and computers, they cannot function as a school without students.
-18. C: A newspaper must have pages to contain its content. Not all newspapers have subscribers, photos, ads, or cartoons, but they all have pages.
-19. D: A bicycle is defined by having two wheels. Not all bicycles have paint, a bell, a basket, or a light, but they all have two wheels.
-20. C: A chair needs legs to stand and support a person. Not all chairs have a cushion, arms, a back, or fabric, but they all need legs.

Verbal Analogies

-21. E: letters put together make up words; sentences put together make up paragraphs
-22. B: feet make a mile; days make a year
-23. A: an enclosed space where dishes are stored is a cabinet; an enclosed space where hay is stored is a barn
-24. D: homophones

Verbal Classification

-25. B: organs found inside body ("organ" is not correct, because it must be a <u>type</u> of organ)
-26. E: types of non-fiction   -27. A: verbs having to do with ending/concluding something
-28. C: adjectives meaning not alike

Verbal Matrix

-29. E. In the first row, "pest" is formed by keeping the "p" and "e", taking the "s" from the second set and adding "t". (The third letter is removed.) In the second row, "mu" and "ms" combine the same way: keep the "m" and "u", take the "s" from the second word and add "t" to make "must".
-30. D: In the first row, "dine" is formed by keeping the "d" and "i", and then taking the "n" from the second set, adding "e". (The third letter is removed.) In the second row, keep the "h", add "i", and take the "v" from the second set and add "e" to make "hive".
-31. C: In the first row, "some" is formed by keeping "so", adding "m", and completing the word with an "e." (The third letter is removed.) In the second row, "go" and "gn" combine the same way to form "gone".
-32. A: down the columns, the top word & bottom word are opposites

Inferences

-33. E: Since all tigers are cats and all cats are animals, it follows that all tigers are both cats and animals. This conclusion is a combination of both statements.
-34. D: To solve this, let's create an ordered list based on the given information. We can summarize the sentences using "greater than" (>) and "less than" (<).
Liam has fewer books than Oliver: Oliver > Liam
Oliver has more books than Emma: Oliver > Emma; So the order is: Oliver > Liam, Emma
-35. C: Mark ran more miles than John: Mark > John
Lisa ran fewer miles than Kevin, but more than Mark: Kevin > Lisa > Mark
Kevin ran more miles than John: Kevin > John
Now we combine the lists: Kevin > Lisa > Mark > John

Figure Analogies

-36. C: original shape rotates 180 degrees & another identical shape is added
-37. E: shapes change like this: ovals become smiley faces, smiley faces become ovals, pentagons become dollar signs & vice versa
-38. B: all shapes switch color gray to black/black to gray; smallest center shape & large outer shape switch positions; middle shape becomes smaller
-39. D: shape with +1 side appears

Figure Series

-40. A: 3 gray circles rotate clockwise around the shape group
-41. D: In each group, there are 3 arch shapes. In the first box, 2 arches point left & 1 arch points right. In each box, the arch that points right moves over 1 position. Also, the wavy line switches from bottom to top.

Pattern Matrix

-42. A: across rows, the figure rotates 90°clockwise
-43. E: across rows & down columns, the shapes from the first two boxes combine in the third box and stay in the same position
-44. C: a small gray shape moves clockwise around the quarters of the square; as it moves it switches between a heart and a star

ANSWER KEY FOR PRACTICE TEST 1 (WORKBOOK FORMAT), CONTINUED

Numeric Matrix

-45. C: across rows, subtract 12; down columns, add 6
-46. A: across rows, 17 is added to the first number to get the second number, then 7 is added to get the third number (+17,+7); down columns, 5 is subtracted
-47. D: across rows, 3 is subtracted from the first number to get the second number, then 5 is subtracted to get the third number (-3, -5); down columns, 4 is subtracted from the first number to get the second number, then 2 is subtracted to get the third number (-4, -2).
-48. D: across rows, 5 is added to the first number to get the second number, then 9 is added to get the third number (+5, +9); down columns, 6 is added to the first number to get the second number, then 3 is subtracted to get the third number (+6, -3)

Numeric Inferences

-49. E: +225   -50. D: +9, -6
-51. E: the second number is the number in the tens position in the first number
-52. E: +21, -10

Numeric Series

-53. D: -1, -2, -1, -2, continues -OR- every other number is 3 less
-54. E: +1, +1, +2; +1, +1, +2, continues
-55. C: begins with 9, every other number is 9; then, starting with 25, every other number is +5
-56. C: the numbers in spaces 1, 3, 5, 7, 9 increase by 1; the numbers in spaces 2, 4, 6, 8, 10 increase by 1 -OR- the difference in each pair of numbers is 11 (20 & 9; 21 & 10; 22 & 11, etc.)

ANSWER KEY FOR PRACTICE TEST 2
- Note: At the end of each explanation is the OLSAT® question type in gray font (Antonyms, Sentence Arrangement, Arithmetic Reasoning, Figure Analogies, etc.).

-1. B. Instant means happening immediately. Gradual means taking place slowly. Antonyms
-2. B. Correct sentence: Being kind to others helps build strong friendships. Sentence Arrangement
-3. B. Samantha scored 10 goals, and Jake scored 12 goals. 10 + 12 = 22 Arithmetic Reasoning
-4. C. shapes align vertically then switch colors Figure Analogies
-5. E. Ascend means to go up or climb. Descend means to go down or move lower. Antonyms
-6. B. A library must have books to serve its main purpose. Logical Selection
-7. D. things under the ground Verbal Classification
-8. E. team/person one is competing against Verbal Classification
-9. E. Julia has fewer apples than Kate: Kate > Julia
Lucas has more apples than Mike, but fewer than Julia: Julia > Lucas > Mike
We can combine the lists as: Kate > Julia > Lucas > Mike Inferences
-10. E. Correct sentence: Telling the truth builds trust with your friends. Sentence Arrangement
-11. B. First, Lily gave 5 marbles to Tom. Then, Tom received 2 more marbles from Alex. 5 + 2 = 7 Arithmetic Reasoning
-12. C. middle shape gets bigger, then top shape gets bigger & moves inside this shape, then bottom shape moves to the center of these two shapes and flips 180 degrees Figure Analogies

-13. B. across rows: ÷2, +4; down columns: the same number that's added to go from the top to the middle number is added again to go from the middle to the bottom number (in column 1, it's +4, +4; in column 2, it's +2, +2; in column 3, it's +2, +2) Numeric Matrix

-14. E. disagreement: a situation where people argue about something or have different opinions Sentence Completion

-15. A. In the first row, "clock" is formed by combining "cl" and "ck" and adding an "o" in the middle. In the second row, "bl" and "bk" combine the same way to form "block". Verbal Matrix

-16. B. Essential means necessary/important. Unnecessary means not necessary. Antonyms

-17. B. equivalent: the same Sentence Completion

-18. C. -45, then -21 Numeric Inferences

-19. C. Correct sentence: Learning from mistakes helps you improve. Sentence Arrangement

-20. A. If Ben gives all but 5 apples to Chloe, this means that Ben keeps 5 apples and gives the rest to Chloe. Since we are asked how many apples Ben has (and not Chloe), the correct response should be 5, not 20. Arithmetic Reasoning

-21. C. A house must have walls to enclose it. Not every house has windows, lights, electricity, or a kitchen. Logical Selection

-22. B. old-fashioned tool > modern tool to perform similar task (measuring time > doing math) Verbal Analogies

-23. D. object > name of the middle of this object Verbal Analogies

-24. E. Correct sentence: Respecting others shows that you care about them. Sentence Arrangement

-25. A. A train must have an engine to move. Logical Selection

-26. E. both are precious metals > both are gases Verbal Analogies

-27. A. synonyms Verbal Analogies

-28. C. across the rows, use letters 1, 2, and 4; replace the 3rd letter with an "o" Verbal Matrix

-29. A. Reveal means to make something known/to tell. Conceal means to hide something or keep it secret. Antonyms

-30. E. compact: not taking up a lot of space/tightly packed together Sentence Completion

-31. D. The flight was scheduled to depart at 3:00 PM, but it was delayed until 3:45 PM, meaning it was 45 minutes late (3:45 - 3:00 = 45 minutes). Since Sofia arrived 30 minutes early, she waited those 30 minutes until the flight was supposed to depart, plus the additional 45 minutes because of the delay. Therefore, Sofia waited a total of: 30 + 45 = 75 minutes. Arithmetic Reasoning

-32. B. Every river has had water at some time. It might be dried up or it could have running water. Logical Selection

-33. C. +2.0 Numeric Series

-34. B. Ancestor means a family member from the past, like a great-grandparent. Descendant means a person in future generations, like a child or grandchild. Antonyms

-35. D. contaminates: makes something dirty or polluted Sentence Completion

-36. A. enclosed places meant for storage Verbal Classification

-37. D. a geographical location with borders Verbal Classification

-38. E. -1, -1, +3; -1, -1, +3, continues Number Series

-39. B. every number repeats itself and then decreases by 2 Numeric Series

-40. A. All words end with -ight and "sight" is the only choice with this ending. Verbal Matrix

-41. C. shapes change like this: rectangles & triangles switch, ovals stay the same Figure Analogies

-42. B. a wrapper protects gum; bark protects a pine (tree type) Verbal Analogies

-43. C. -1, -2, -3, -4, -5, etc. Numeric Series

-44. B. down the columns, the words begin with the same letter Verbal Matrix

-45. D. bottom shape becomes top shape & gets smaller, middle shape becomes bottom shape & gets bigger, top shape becomes middle shape & gets bigger Figure Analogies

ANSWER KEY FOR PRACTICE TEST 2, CONTINUED

-46. D. +15, then -6 Numeric Inferences

-47. C. +2, +7, -1, repeats Numeric Series

-48. C. across rows: -11, -5; down columns: +10, +2 Numeric Matrix

-49. A. The diagonal line dividing the circle switches from going upper left to lower right & lower left to upper right. Also, the design/color in the circle half that faces the next circle is "mirrored" in the circle next to it. From box 1 to 2, it's dotted lines. From box 2 to 3, it's horizontal lines. From 3 to 4, it's white. From 4 to 5 (the answer), it's dotted lines. Finally, in the other half of the circle (the half that does not have this "mirror" design), the design must be different than the circle that came before it. From box 1 to 2, it changes from white to horizontal lines. From box 2 to 3, it changes from dotted lines to white. From box 3 to 4, it changes from horizontal lines to dotted lines. From box 4 to 5, it changes from white to horizontal lines. Figure Series

-50. E. across rows: +5, +7; down columns: -3, +12 Numeric Matrix

-51. D. bottom shape goes to top as the top shape goes to bottom & rotates 180° Figure Series

-52. D. across rows: x3; down columns: x4 Numeric Matrix

-53. E. Each box has one dotted heart (the rest are white). In each box, the dotted heart moves back one position (4-3-2-1). So, after it's in position 1, it must go back to 4. Figure Series

-54. E. the circles in the right column must have all three designs: white, gray, and horizontal lines as a larger outer circle is added to the previous 2 circles Pattern Matrix

-55. B. in each box, the number of hearts & number of "pac-man" shapes decrease by 1, the number of circles increases by 1 Figure Series

-56. B. the final column has 3 shapes: a large, small, and medium sized version; the small shape is in the upper right corner; the middle shape is in front of the larger shape on the left side of the box -or- the middle shape is the same shape as the larger shape in the 2nd column Pattern Matrix

-57. A. across rows: inside the square sections, the diamond moves around clockwise & the rectangle changes position in the second box, but in the third box it returns to its original position Pattern Matrix

-58. B. 2 sections with gray move counterclockwise around the divided rectangle Figure Series

-59. C. x4, then +4 Numeric Inferences

-60. E. across the rows the 2 shapes that appear in a box with only 2 shapes (square & oval; "pac-man" & cross; parallelogram & arrow) must always appear together in same order; across the rows, shapes must change color (this makes C incorrect); a box in each row must combine the three shapes Pattern Matrix

-61. D. across each row shapes have the same number of sides (down each column the number of shape sides increases by 1); across rows & down columns each shape is a different color & each square is a different color Pattern Matrix

-62. D. ÷3, then +4 Numeric Inferences

-63. A. Tom is taller than Emily: Tom > Emily; Emily is shorter than Rachel: Rachel > Emily
From this, we know that Tom and Rachel are both taller than Emily. Inferences

-64. E. Liam has more pencils than Emma: Liam > Emma
Noah has more pencils than James: Noah > James
Oliver has fewer pencils than Emma but more pencils than James: Emma > Oliver > James
Now, Liam > Emma > Oliver > James -and- Noah > James
From this, we can conclude that James has the fewest pencils. Inferences

-65. C: Sophia is shorter than Mason: Mason > Sophia
    Lily is taller than Jack, but shorter than Sophia: Sophia > Lily > Jack
    When you combine the two: Mason > Sophia > Lily > Jack; So, Lily is shorter than Mason.
    Inferences

-66. D: subtle: hard to see, not obvious Sentence Completion
-67. A: negotiate: to discuss something so that an agreement can be made Sentence Completion
-68. D: modify: to change Sentence Completion
-69. B: inhabitants: someone who lives in a particular place Sentence Completion
-70. C: +2.5 Numeric Series

ANSWER KEY FOR PRACTICE TEST 3

- Note: At the end of each explanation is the OLSAT® question type in gray font (Antonyms, Sentence Arrangement, Arithmetic Reasoning, Figure Analogies, etc.).

-1. C. Blossom means to grow or flourish, especially in terms of plants. Wither means to dry up or lose life. Antonyms
-2. E. Each box has 12 crayons, and if you buy 5 boxes, multiply 5 × 12 = 60. Arithmetic Reasoning
-3. E. the number in spaces 1, 3, 5, 7 double; the numbers in spaces 2, 4, 6 double, etc. Number Series Number Series
-4. D. +34, +34 Numeric Inferences
-5. D. Coax means to gently persuade or encourage. Force means to make someone do something without choice. Antonyms
-6. A. Add all the apples Lily picked and subtract all the apples she used or gave away. On Monday, she picked 18 apples. On Wednesday, she gave away 4 apples, so: 18 - 4 = 14.
On Friday, she picked 6 apples and used 5 apples for the pie: 14 + 6 - 5 = 15.
On Sunday, she picked 7 apples and gave away 3 apples: 15 + 7 - 3 = 19. Arithmetic Reasoning
-7. D. a hoof is the foot of a giraffe; a paw is the foot of a rabbit Verbal Analogies
-8. E. -7 Numeric Inferences
-9. E. Distress means a state of suffering or worry. Relief means feeling calm and free from worry. Antonyms
-10. D. in the sections of the squares/parallelograms, the colors/designs change like this: gray becomes filled with lines, black becomes gray, and sections filled with lines become black; also, the original figures do not change their shapes Figure Analogies
-11. A. +8, then -6 Numeric Inferences
-12. B. across rows: -25, +23; down columns: +36, -17 Numeric Matrix
-13. C. Appropriate means suitable or fitting. Improper means not suitable or wrong. Antonyms
-14. E. middle shape becomes the largest outer shape; then, the top shape becomes the 2nd largest shape and moves inside the largest shape; then, the bottom shape moves inside both of these shapes, rotates 90° counterclockwise & turns gray Figure Analogies
-15. B. x6 Numeric Inferences
-16. E. -8, -7, -6, -5, -4, etc. Numeric Series
-17. B. Saying kind words can brighten someone's day. Sentence Arrangement
-18. D. A farm requires land to grow crops or raise animals. Logical Selection
-19. D. In te + im = time, let's assign each letter a number: t = 1, e = 2, i = 3, m = 4.
In the 3rd column, the pattern is: 1 + 3 + 4 + 2.
In et + di = ?, let's also assign each letter a number: e = 1, t = 2, d = 3, i = 4. Remember the pattern: 1 + 3 + 4 + 2. So, the new word is e + d + i + t = edit. Verbal Matrix
-20. D. x2 then +1 Numeric Inferences
-21. A. Correct sentence: The student who started the recycling program received an award. Sentence Arrangement
-22. E. impacts = effect; ability = having the means to do something/to be able to do something Sentence Completion

-23. C. A zoo must have animals. Not every zoo has lions, a map, visitors, or even cages, but all zoos have animals. Logical Selection

-24. E. ÷2 then +1 Numeric Inferences

-25. E. Correct sentence: Grandma took us to a bakery where we bought cupcakes. Sentence Arrangement

-26. C. result in = cause to happen; alternative = something that's possible as another choice Sentence Completion

-27. C. "Seven less than four times five, plus three" can be written as: (4 × 5) - 7 + 3 = 16. Arithmetic Reasoning

-28. A. Every mountain has a peak, which is its highest point. Logical Selection

-29. D. "Simple" means easy to understand, basic, or plain. "Complex" means not easy to understand; complicated. Antonyms

-30. A. Kites have strings that keep them steady in the wind. Sentence Arrangement

-31. B. potential = to have or show the ability to make something in the future; generate = produce Sentence Completion

-32. B. "Ten more than three times eight, minus six" can be written as: (3 × 8) + 10 - 6 = 28. Arithmetic Reasoning

-33. A. Every mountain must have a summit (the mountain's highest point). Mountains may have the other things, but they are not necessary. Logical Selection

-34. B. digits decrease by 1 (i.e., from 51 to 50 to 50 to 49, etc.) -AND- the signs alternate between positive and negative Numeric Series

-35. E. A sock is a protective covering for a foot. An atmosphere is a protective covering for a planet (such as Earth). Verbal Analogies

-36. B. This is an example of "degree." Something very dim is dark. Something very cool is frigid. Verbal Analogies

-37. E. used to carry/hold things Verbal Classification

-38. C. used to describe sizes Verbal Classification

-39. B. In the first row, "steam" is formed by combining "st" and "am" and adding "e" in between. In the second row, "dr" and "am" and inserting "e" form "dream". Verbal Matrix

-40. A. There is cooperation between partners and competition between opponents. Verbal Analogies

-41. E. Drought is caused by a lack of rain. Hunger is caused by a lack of food. Verbal Analogies

-42. B. verbs having to do with bringing things together Verbal Classification

-43. C. things that happen at the beginning of something Verbal Classification

-44. C. down the columns, the top word has a short vowel of the word's first letter & the bottom word has a long vowel of the word's first letter Verbal Matrix

-45. B. down the columns, the top word is used to measure the bottom word Verbal Matrix

-46. E. the shape group rotates 90° clockwise, then the gray circles become black and vice versa Figure Analogies

-47. C. light gray shape 'flips' down, dark gray shape added on top that's facing the original position of the first shape Figure Analogies

-48. D. -1,-1,+1; -3,-3,+3; -4,-4,+4 Numeric Series

-49. D. down columns, top is the animal class & bottom is an animal in that class Verbal Matrix

-50. A. the triangle with horizontal stripes becomes solid gray; the black triangle remains black; the triangle with dotted lines remains with dotted lines; then, the group of 3 triangles rotates 180° Figure Analogies

-51. B. you magnify with a lens; you cut with a blade Verbal Analogies

-52. A. across rows: -21; down columns: -9 Numeric Matrix

-53. D. top shape moves to the bottom Figure Series

-54. E. across rows: ÷3, ÷2; down columns: ÷3, x2 Numeric Matrix
-55. D. across rows: -8, +4; down columns: -11, +6 Numeric Matrix
-56. D. across rows, gray rectangle moves clockwise once around group of circles Pattern Matrix
-57. A. in every box, the triangle rotates clockwise to the next section of the cross -and- changes direction (pointing up vs. pointing down); also, in every other box, the octagon rotates clockwise to the next section of the cross Figure Series
-58. B. white wand rotates 45° clockwise; in 2 of the 3 boxes there will be one gray wand which always lays on top of the white wand; gray wand rotates 90° counterclockwise from the first box to the second box in which it appears Pattern Matrix
-59. E. across rows is 1 of each: color of large square (dark gray/light gray/white), type & color of middle shape (hexagon/trapezoid/diamond) (dark gray/light gray/white), type & color of smaller shape (hexagon/trapezoid/diamond) (dark gray/light gray/white) Pattern Matrix
-60. C. multiply by 3 Numeric Series
-61. B. square moves to the right across the boxes; row must have a small triangle, medium triangle, large triangle; note that in the middle row, middle box the square covers the triangle Pattern Matrix
-62. A. in each box, the upper left square adds another line, which divides it further into eighths -and- a small square in the lower right is removed Figure Series
-63. E. add 19 Numeric Series
-64. C. James runs faster than Lily: James > Lily
Zoe runs faster than Max but not as fast as Kate: Kate > Zoe > Max
James runs faster than Max but not as fast as Zoe: Zoe > James > Max
Therefore, it is clear that Kate runs the fastest. Inferences
-65. B.
Sarah runs faster than Amy: Sarah > Amy
Amy runs faster than Emma but slower than Olivia: Olivia > Amy > Emma
From this, we have Sarah/Olivia > Amy > Emma.
Since we don't know how Sarah compares to Olivia directly, there are two possible ways that could be ordered: Sarah > Olivia > Amy > Emma OR Olivia > Sarah > Amy > Emma
In either case, Emma runs the slowest. Inferences
-66. C. -9, +8, -2, repeats Numeric Series
-67. B. large shape rotates 180 degrees; smaller shapes switch color Figure Analogies
-68. B. words where the letters are put in reverse order to form another word Verbal Analogies
-69. E. a sleeve extends out of a jacket; a branch extends out of a tree Verbal Analogies
-70. A. geography is a type of social studies; biology is a type of science Verbal Analogies

Ready for test day?

Check out more OLSAT® books at

www.GatewayGifted.com

Grade 3

Grade 2